THE FAST MEN

Brown of Brighton had men trembling as long
ago as 1820; Alfred Mynn and John Jackson,
and later Richardson and Lockwood, were
champions of the 19th century; Kortright was
possibly the fastest of all time; Australia's
impressive line began with Spofforth 'the
Demon' and Jones, and has continued through
Gregory and McDonald, Lindwall and Miller,
and today by Thompson and Lillee; West
Indies have always had plenty of fast men
like Constantine, Hall and Griffith, and now
Roberts and Holding; South Africa
slaughtered Australia in their final Test
series before isolation, chiefly through
Procter and Pollock, the fiery successors of
Adcock and Heine; some of England's greatest
successes have been sparked off by Larwood,
Tyson, Statham, Trueman and Snow.
The stories of all these and many more are
embodied in this book. How does an express
bowler see his function, and where does he
find his inspiration? Quite as fascinating:
what passes through a batsman's mind when
faced with this physical peril? The answers
are in *The Fast Men*.

The Fast Men

A 200-year cavalcade of speed bowlers

David Frith

Preface by
JOHN ARLOTT

CORGI BOOKS
A DIVISION OF TRANSWORLD PUBLISHERS LTD

THE FAST MEN

A CORGI BOOK 0 552 10435 3

Originally published in Great Britain
by Van Nostrand Reinhold Company Limited

PRINTING HISTORY

Van Nostrand Reinhold Company Limited edition published 1975
Corgi revised and up-dated edition published 1977

This book is set in Pilgrim 10/11 pt.

Corgi Books are published by Transworld Publishers, Ltd.,
Century House, 61–63 Uxbridge Road, Ealing,
London, W5 5SA

Made and Printed in Great Britain by
Richard Clay (The Chaucer Press), Ltd., Bungay, Suffolk

CONTENTS

ACKNOWLEDGEMENTS

My thanks are extended to John Arlott, for kindly undertaking to write the Preface; to Patrick Eager, for assisting in the preparation of the photographs; to the various copyright-holders, for permission to use their photographs; to Irving Rosenwater, for running a precautionary eye over the proofs; to Richard Smart for his perception in January, encouragement in March, and tolerance in June; and to the Fast Men of my lifetime, for inflicting so many nasty-but-nice stomach tremors.

DAVID FRITH

For Peter, who in time may join them;
John, who may have to resist them;
and Julie may she never marry one.

PREFACE

by John Arlott

All the best ideas, it is said, are simple. So, the first reaction to this book is to wonder why on earth it was not written years ago. The fast bowler is the most colourful character in cricket but all too little print has been devoted to the breed.

The batsmen—W. G. Grace, Gilbert Jessop, Jack Hobbs, Don Bradman, Wally Hammond, Denis Compton—are generally regarded as the players who filled cricket grounds. Yet it is difficult to believe that other people besides the writer did not go to see, and be stirred by, fast bowlers. Surely they paid to watch Tom Richardson, Charles Kortright, Neville Knox, Gregory and McDonald as later generations did to see Harold Larwood, Learie Constantine, Ken Farnes, Miller and Lindwall, Fred Trueman, Tyson and Statham, and last of all Thomson, Lillee, and Roberts.

It is true that many people have been fascinated to watch men build up vast mountains of runs, grinding bowlers under the bat. Certainly, cricket grounds in Australia used almost to empty when Don Bradman was out. There has always, though, been an opposite kind of pleasure. No-one who experienced it will ever forget the sharp intake of breath all round a cricket ground when people saw Tyson bowl for the first time. There is no more savagely moving experience than to be part of a crowd watching a fast bowler—better still, a pair of fast bowlers—knocking down wickets. When the pitch is fast, or 'green'—preferably both —and batsmen are being tumbled out, the temper of the crowd becomes almost primitive. Each time a wicket falls, the killer howl goes up. When the process is constant it

9

seems that the cry is kept, on a delicate trigger, in the throat so that it is released almost before the batsman knows he is out.

Fast bowling is a dual experience. It may be that of identification with the bowler in his basically fierce attack. Others identify with the batsman; no situation in any sport—except perhaps that of the bullfighter—is lonelier than his. Cricket is a team game; yet its main performances are not simply individual but completely isolated. Such is the position—and the need—of both the fast bowler and his batsman opponent.

The title of 'fastest of them all' passes from generation to generation. The first holder of it, of course, was the legendary Brown of Brighton, who bowled the ball that beat the bat, wicket, wicketkeeper, long stop, went through a man's coat on the boundary and killed a dog on the other side. In the 1890s the mantle settled—and long remained—on Charles Kortright of Essex, an amateur cricketer if ever there was one. Asked one day 'What did you *do*, Charles?' he answered:

'What do you mean, *do*—?'

'Well, you know, for a living?'

'Didn't have to earn a living, father left enough for me and my sister.'

'Well what did you do except bowl fast?'

'Bowled leg-breaks and played golf.'

Once he recalled the historic Gentlemen v Players match of 1898, begun on W. G. Grace's fiftieth birthday, July 18. He and 'the Old Man' had fallen out some years before during a match at Leyton when 'Korty' hit WG in the stomach with a lifter from a slow pitch. The morning, Charles said, 'was so hot it was difficult to get from the Great Eastern Hotel, where I had stayed, to Lord's. The heat was so great that horses were collapsing between the shafts of the hansom cabs and the streets were blocked with them. We started at midday. Jacker (F. S. Jackson) and I opened the bowling. We went along pretty well; I bowled Bobby

Abel, and Arthur Shrewsbury just shut up his end. About one, the Old Man came up to me—and he hadn't spoken to me for at least four years—and said:

'Can you go on Korty?'

'Yes,' I said, 'if you want me to Doctor'—so I bowled until lunch at half past one.' Kortright, according to the records, bowled well with no luck. Like all bowlers, though, he had an urge to bat and it was one of the proudest memories of his life that he and WG—who came in late because of an injury—put on 78 for the last wicket and failed to save the game by only a couple of minutes; and Korty's 46 was the highest score of the innings.

In every generation the old stories are told about new bowlers. Those credited to Richardson, Kortright and Lockwood in England, Jones and Gregory in Australia, have passed down to Larwood, McCormick, Lindwall and Trueman. Fast bowlers are the stuff of cricket mythology. Here they are recorded with evocative accuracy.

David Frith was a 'natural' to write this book. Born in England, brought up in Australia, returning to England—where he became editor of *The Cricketer*—and with a considerable feeling for West Indian cricket, he was as nearly an unbiased author as one could have hoped to find for such a theme. His enthusiastic study of the game has put the material ready into his hands. He has obviously enjoyed writing this history as much as we shall enjoy reading it.

J.A.

1. BLACK TUESDAY

Ewen Chatfield's narrow escape
Dennis Lillee and Jeff Thomson destroy England
role of the umpire—injury follows injury

On Sunday, February 23, 1975, at Eden Park, Auckland, New Zealand were slipping gently towards an innings defeat by England. With nine second-innings wickets down, they still trailed by 127 runs when last man Chatfield joined Geoff Howarth with half an hour left. Had Chris Old been fit to bowl and had Tony Greig's spinning finger not been troubling him England would in all likelihood have finished the game that afternoon. But Howarth and Chatfield held out, adding 21 academic runs, and the game was extended beyond the rest day to resumption on the Tuesday morning.

That fateful morning saw further stubborn resistance—irritating resistance to England's bowlers, one of whom, Peter Lever of Lancashire, knowing the discomfiture a short, fast ball would cause a number eleven batsman, and having come close already to having Chatfield caught off his glove, utilised the device which suggested itself from among a professional fast bowler's repertoire. He 'dug the ball in'. It reared. Chatfield, behind the line of it, was helpless. It touched his glove and struck him on the temple. He staggered from the wicket and fell moaning, legs twitching, face turning purple. For three or four seconds his heart stopped. He swallowed his tongue.

Had it not been for the immediate attention of MCC

physiotherapist Bernard Thomas and St John's Ambulance officer, John Hayland, who applied mouth-to-mouth resuscitation and heart massage, Ewen Chatfield, a 24-year-old industrial chemist from Wellington, playing his first Test match, would almost certainly have become modern first-class cricket's first fast-bowling fatality.

The irony of this tragedy was that England had just crossed the Tasman Sea after a disastrous campaign in Australia, where Jeff Thomson and Dennis Lillee had bombarded, bruised and humiliated them in five of the six Test matches. The last Test England won by an innings, supplying proof if it were needed that Australia owed almost everything to their two express bowlers, now absent through injury. England had gone to Australia armed with five fast or fastish bowlers and with their intentions fairly clear. The Ashes had been won in 1970–71 largely through John Snow's fast bowling: the techniques of several key Australian batsmen were found lacking against the short-pitched ball. Now, four years later, Mike Denness's side harboured hopes that three or four out of Willis, Old, Lever, Hendrick and Arnold, conceivably with Greig in his faster style (Snow was overlooked altogether, to howls of condemnation from the masses), would repeat the performance. Before the series started there were grave doubts that Lillee's back injury was completely cured and scepticism at reports that Australia had unearthed another 'demon' in Jeff Thomson.

Yet the series was a walkover for Ian Chappell's Australians, Thomson blasting his way to 33 wickets in five Tests at an average of under 18, and Lillee, getting faster as the season developed, taking 25 at 23·84. Three England bowlers took 17 wickets each, and only one, Willis, was a fast man. The wretched Peter Lever took none for 111 at Brisbane in the first Test and failed to gain selection again until the final Test, at Melbourne. There, generally keeping the ball well up to the batsman and gaining movement as a result, he confounded those who had written him off by taking 6 for 38 on the first day, when Australia, negligently choosing to bat, were put out for 152. He took three more in the second innings, and symbolically finished off the match by bowling Australia's last man. At 34 he was perhaps not the spent force most critics suspected. The selectors' faith had been justified. It had been unfair, after all, to suggest that his un-doubted aggression over a mere twelve overs in Gillette Cup matches in 1974 was no proof of his stamina for a five-day Test match (though his eleven overs on that glorious first day at Melbourne took their toll). One delivery had reared to strike Greg Chappell painfully on the jaw. Against all the odds, Lever, when by rights he ought to have been quietly packing his bags for a hushed return to England, had become his country's spearhead. Then came Auckland.

As Chatfield lay prone on the pitch and England's cricketers stood around helplessly and in various states of distress, Lever, on his haunches, wept. He was certain he had killed the batsman. He wanted to retire there and then.

Later he told an *Evening Standard* reporter : 'I don't want any bloody sympathy, do you understand that? It has hap-pened. People who say "I know how you feel" are just talking bullshit. They don't know. Not at all. What I can't forget is that the ball was a deliberate short one. Not deliber-ately at his head, but still deliberate.'

Chatfield recovered consciousness an hour later in hospi-tal and before long was expressing a determination to get back into cricket. But the accident cost him any chance he may have had of taking part in the World Cup in England four months later. He gallantly exonerated Lever, gingerly touching the closed fracture and telling reporters that it was not really the bowler's fault. Not even the bowler him-self could take that seriously.

Lever was persuaded to play in the remaining Test match, at Christchurch, and in a match dogged by bad weather he began with a wide, bowled barely a ball short of a length, and was applauded warmly by an understanding crowd. Chatfield, five days after his brush with death, sat in the stand, having been flown to the match at the expense of the New Zealand Cricket Council.

By now letters were flying in all directions: to *The Times*, *The Daily Telegraph*, *The Cricketer*, and the popular news-papers. Ban the bouncer! Paint a line across the pitch! Allow batsmen to wear crash-helmets! Award ten runs against the bowler for a short-pitched delivery! Send him off! The British Safety Council urged the Minister for Sport to incorporate cricket fields into the scope of the new Health and Safety Act. The Snell Memorial Foundation of California, broadening its specific purpose 'to aid, help, promote and insure the life, safety, well being and comfort of persons participating in or about any type of travel or vehicular transportation', came down heavily in favour of protective headgear, citing research by Dr R. W. Cockshut, a former chairman of The Cricket Society, into fatalities in minor cricket from head blows. To this suggestion, echoed else-where, cricketers and cricket-lovers almost unanimously raised their hands in horror, suspecting that such procedure would merely serve as licence to fast bowlers to aim at the head. Only one baseball batter had ever been killed by a pitch, and thanks to Chatfield's recovery cricket (first-class) maintained a clean sheet since George Summers's death in 1870. (In 1959 Abdul Aziz, playing at Karachi, died after being hit below the heart by a ball well short of top pace, but he had a known heart condition.)

No—there was a Law, and it was felt by some players and observers during the 1974–75 Australia v England series that it was not enforced by the Australian umpires as it should have been. Willis and Lever began bumping the ball at Brisbane on November 29, and when England batted Lillee and Thomson took the aggression to new heights—or depths, depending on one's appetite in these matters. Lord Mayor Clem Jones had defeated his critics by creating a Test pitch out of a lake of mud, but the bounce throughout was un-even, and batting against real pace was never anything but a precarious pastime. A surprise feature—developing as the series proceeded—was the bowling of bouncers at tailenders, the fast bowlers themselves and other numbers eight, nine, ten and eleven. Some of the loudest thumps came from balls hitting chests, hips and backs of men like Arnold, Willis, Lillee and Mallett. Some of the narrowest escapes from facial injury came when the lower-order batsmen were at the crease. The first warning came in the first innings of the first Test, when Lever let three in a row fly at Terry Jenner, an obstinate and often hard-hitting number eight, who had been floored bloodily by Snow in the final Test of the 1970–71 series. Now, four years later, the umpire warned Lever. But if this were interpreted as the forerunner of firm jurisdiction during the series it was to be a misinterpretation.

The umpires were Robin Bailhache, standing in his first Tests, and Tom Brooks, an experienced umpire who had opened the bowling with Keith Miller for club and State. As the violent and often foul-mouthed series of 1974–75 played itself remorselessly out there was never more than a muttered reminder, wagged finger or facial expression not without ambivalence from either umpire as the bouncer war feared by so many reached a fierce pitch. England batsmen were moving out of the line of the flying ball and waving feebly at it as it sped over the off stump. Greig and Knott slashed, frequently gathering four runs into the third man fence. Others were caught off the glove or off edges thick and thin, as if conducting fielding practice for the slips and gullies. To Lillee they often managed to duck; to Thomson, with his deceptive slinging action, the ball appearing late from behind his pivoting body, there was hardly time to sight the ball, let alone hook it or duck it. His added venom came from an ability to obtain lift from a fuller-than-usual length. It is doubtful if even the greatest of batsmen, given a series or two, could ever grow accustomed to this form of attack. It was England's one consolation that they could look back to 1954–55 when Frank Tyson with his almost supernatural speed reduced some eminent Australian batsmen to near-impotence. Firmer umpiring in 'Thomson's series' may well have adjusted matters rather more the batsmen's way. But that was not the way it was, and the Australian crowds, who turned up in vast numbers and tended to be younger than usual, loved it all. The chanting

17

from the outer, especially that addressed to Dennis Lillee as he walked back to his mark, turned, and stormed in for another assault on a 'Pommie' batsman, could only have lifted him, as the Liverpool Kop have lifted their footballers to a one- or two-goal moral advantage all these years.

Dennis Amiss and John Edrich suffered broken hands in the first Test; Thomson damaged Luckhurst's knuckle and hit David Lloyd a cruel blow in the pit of the stomach in the second Test; Lloyd's finger was split and Titmus was almost maimed by a ball from Thomson which cannoned into his knee in the third Test; Underwood was hit resoundingly in the ribs by Lillee, who also bowled a beamer at Willis and was cautioned by the umpire after two withering bumpers at Amiss; Fletcher headed an 'unplayable' ball from Thomson to cover point, and John Edrich, dropping earthwards from his first ball from Lillee, suffered broken ribs in the fourth Test (which gave Australia the Ashes); and just for a change Walker inflicted a painful blow on Denness's box in the fifth Test. Jim Laker, the former England off-spinner turned BBC TV commentator, saw several of the Test matches, and stated that the most vicious ball he had seen in his lengthy life in cricket was the bumper let loose first ball by Lillee to tail-ender Geoff Arnold. It parted his hair as he stood frozen and helpless. 'Ray Lindwall,' Laker said, 'never bowled a bouncer at me. He said that if he couldn't bowl out a number nine then he oughtn't to be playing for Australia.'

Jeff Thomson injured himself playing tennis during the fifth Test and Lillee damaged a foot after bowling only six overs in the sixth Test, so shell-shocked England somehow transformed themselves into a well-knit eleven at Melbourne and walked off with the most decisive victory of the series. Posterity will give them only polite credit for this.

So, it was the irony of ironies that, having reached the relative peacefulness of New Zealand, England should have become embroiled in the sickening Lever–Chatfield incident. One columnist even went so far as to blame it upon Ian Chappell, who had encouraged his bowlers to hurl every piece of heavy ammunition they could find during the Australian series so long as the umpires allowed.

There seems one certainty: men have been firing cricket balls with evil intent at other men since long before young Neville Cardus was boiling type in a printer's works. Through the periods of heaviest bombardment sensitive folk have said time and again, 'Someone will be killed some day'. The magic touch of a medical man narrowly averted such a calamity at Eden Park, Auckland on February 25, 1975. But the entire cricket world paused nervously and began a self-examination.

2. THE WONDER OF HARRIS

Lumpy Stevens—David Harris—Tom Brett—Tom Walker
Bob Robinson's pads—death of the Prince of Wales

High velocity in bowling has always meant initiative for
the bowler, and ever since cricket was first played, whether
casually or on an organised basis, the man with the ball has
had the choice of exercising guile or straight-out aggression.
Almost every child who ever played has tried his hand at
fast bowling, it being the natural thing to do. A large physique is an encouragement—almost a mandate—to bowl
as fast as one can. Yet there is no bar to a small fellow
flinging all his nine, ten or eleven stone into it. Bill Edrich,
of Middlesex and England, was the perfect example of a
man of small stature but massive heart, who hurled himself
into the delivery and generated enough pace and lift to cause
even world-class batsmen concern for a few overs.

In the mists of antiquity bowlers *bowled* the ball, as in
lawn bowls, all along the ground, having as their chief ally
the rough surfaces on which the game was staged. The batsman had a hockey-type bat which was used to sweep against
the rolled ball.

The first major development came during the Hambledon
era, when cricket reached new levels of technique and popu-
larity. In the ranks of the Hambledon club and its opponents
were several skilled bowlers who applied spin to the ball,
'gave it air', and studied flight. Such true underarm bowling
still imposed strict limitations upon the speed through the
air that a bowler with an enforcedly cramped action could

generate, though the crude pitches remained a source of assistance. Edward 'Lumpy' Stevens was a master at selecting a pitch, his businesslike approach having been immortalised in verse:

> For honest Lumpy did allow,
> He ne'er could pitch but o'er a brow.

Those brows brought him, mainly from 'shooters', hundreds upon hundreds of wickets in the 1760s, '70s and '80s, and a degree of security too, for the small, dumpy cricketer was employed first by Mr Porter, a Chertsey, Surrey brewer, and then as a gardener for the Earl of Tankerville at Mount Felix, his estate at Walton-on-Thames.

Lumpy, so named perhaps because of his shape, perhaps because of his ability to dispatch an entire apple pie in next to no time, or perhaps because of a peculiarity in his bowling, won his patron many wagers in team and individual contests, none more famous than by landing the ball on a feather four times in succession at the Burway Ground at Chertsey. His Lordship became £100 richer as a result of that little exercise, and one wonders how many bowlers today would be capable of such accuracy.

To Lumpy, who was said to have been 'a bit of a smuggler' in his younger days, fell the distinction of expediting legislation to have the third stump added. In a match around 1775 he beat the great John Small senior several times only to see the ball pass between the two stumps surmounted by a crosspiece. Consciences were stirred, and evolution took another step forward.

Lumpy's speed was less than that of David Harris, whose lifelong bachelorhood may have enabled him to perfect his craft with long hours of practice in a barn during the winter months and whenever wet weather prevented play. He was a Hampshire man by birth and residence, a potter by trade, and without question the finest bowler of the age. John Nyren in *The Cricketers of My Time*, the classic of 1833, described his action: 'First of all, he stood erect like a soldier at drill; then, with a graceful curve of the arm, he raised the ball to his forehead, and drawing back his right foot, started off with his left. The calm look and general air of the man were uncommonly striking, and from this series of preparations he never deviated.... His mode of delivering the ball was very singular. He would bring it from under the arm by a twist, and nearly as high as his arm-pit, and with this action *push* it, as it were, from him. How it was that the balls acquired the velocity they did by this mode of delivery I could never comprehend.'

In his early days Harris was inclined to bowl a lot of full-tosses, but constant study and practice honed his bowling to near-perfection. A high proportion of his wickets were taken by catches, and by stumpings and hit-wicket. What must also have undermined many of his opponents was the calmness and 'sweetness of his disposition', quite apart from his shrewdness in selecting the ground upon which to pitch the wickets. In this important contemporary strategy he conceded nothing to the scheming Lumpy Stevens.

The finest cricket to be seen in this period was Harris bowling to the champion batsman, 'Silver Billy' Beldham. Of this kind of material cricket historians' dreams are made.

Like many a celebrated fast bowler, David Harris saw out his days in sad circumstances. A victim of gout, he played his last seasons partly couched in a wheelchair, rising only to deliver the ball. He died in his forties and was buried in the churchyard at Crondall—today without trace.

Contemporaries of Lumpy Stevens were John Frame, a very stout fellow and for several years second only to Lumpy in fame, and Thomas 'Shock' White and John Wood, neither of whom was quite in the top flight of bowlers. White's immortality rests in the hilarious affair of his appearing with a bat as wide as the wicket. The Hambledon Club speedily drew up a law limiting the width of the bat, and a gauge was manufactured to see that the law was adhered to!

For sheer speed, Tom Brett, a Catherington farmer, was probably foremost of the Hambledon era. He bowled straight, too, as did Brian Statham two hundred years later, happy in the knowledge that 'if the batsman misses, I hit!' Strong, well-built, and dark, Brett was, according to Nyren, 'neither a thrower nor a jerker, but a legitimate downright bowler, delivering his ball fairly, high, and very quickly, quite as strongly as the jerkers, and with the force of a point blank shot', which seems to imply that suspicious actions were not uncommon. His 'steam-engine bowling' demanded the best in long-stops, and this function was fulfilled admirably by 'Little George' Lear, a 'sand-bank' in that position, who sometimes achieved almost a 'maximum' by keeping losses to a mere two runs in a whole match—this to the 'swiftest bowling ever known'. But the most thrilling spectacle would have been Tom Sueter's wicket-keeping. He actually effected fairly regular stumpings off Brett's fearsome bowling. Nyren wrote fondly: 'What a handful of steel-hearted soldiers are in an important pass, such was Tom in keeping the wicket.'

Brett's successor was Richard Francis, who went to Hambledon from Surrey. He *was* a jerker, though considered fair. He was never in the same class as Brett; he was smaller, a gamekeeper by occupation, but an answer to Hambledon's need. Few teams (the South Africans of 1907, with their googly bowlers, and the Indians of the early 1970s, with their spin quartette, come to mind) have ever asserted themselves without at least one outstanding fast bowler.

Another Surrey man who joined Hambledon was Tom Walker, brother of Harry and John. He owes his place in the story not for any great feats of fast bowling but because he startled his fellows by suddenly bowling (or jerking) roundarm fashion. It was an expression, perhaps, of the restlessness of bowlers who could see beyond the restraints imposed by tradition, and it foreshadowed a revolution.

Walker was brought to heel by the Hambledon committee, who forbade such an action and broadcast their feelings on the matter. 'Old Everlasting' Walker was left to bowl 'underhand lobs of the tedious slow school', and was very

23

successful with them. His nickname came about from his Bill Lawry-type occupation of the crease. He once took 170 balls from David Harris and scored one run from them! If his gloveless knuckles were opened by the impact of the ball he would simply rub the bleeding wound in the dust.

There can seldom have been a more colourful description of a cricketer than Nyren's of Walker, who, frustrated as a fast roundarm bowler, could at least withstand the fieriest of his day: 'Tom's hard, ungain, scrag-of-mutton frame; wilted, apple-john face (he always looked twenty years older than he really was), his long spider legs, as thick at the ankles as at the hips, and perfectly straight all the way down—for the embellishment of a calf in Tom's leg, Dame Nature had considered would be but a wanton superfluity. Tom was the driest and most rigid-limbed chap I ever knew; his skin was like the rind of an old oak, and as sapless. I have seen his knuckles handsomely knocked about from Harris's bowling; but never saw any blood upon his hands—you might just as well attempt to phlebotomize a mummy.... He moved like the rude machinery of a steam-engine in the infancy of construction, and when he ran, every member seemed ready to fly to the four winds.' Hardly the stuff of which fast bowlers are made.

David Harris stands out toweringly from these times. His skill presented batsmen with serious problems which had to be overcome. It had been the order of things that back-play, with plenty of slashing, ensured both survival and runs. Against Harris's pace and lift this was useless, and a generation of forward-playing, cautious batsmen emerged. William Fennex claimed himself as the leader of the batting revival, stretching so far forward that his own father became curious. But it was effective, and when years later the great William Lambert employed similar methods, and later still Fuller Pilch brought forward-play almost to perfection, old Fennex preferred to believe that it was his example passed on, though Beldham's footwork and forward play were original and regarded with awe and admiration.

24

There must have been countless dented shins and bruised toes inflicted by bowlers in the eighteenth century, and Bob Robinson, a 16-stone left-hander from Farnham, did his best to offset this by making leg-guards of thin wood. Sadly the 'clunk' of ball on pad reduced all within earshot to ribald laughter, and the innovation was abandoned. Batsmen (who, incidentally, only ever had their legs hit by accident in those days) were destined to weather a good many more seasons with vulnerable shins, with Frederick Louis, Prince of Wales, one of the few fatalities known by name. In 1751 the Prince, Surrey's first recorded captain, was hit in the side by a cricket ball (Horace Walpole wrote that it was a tennis ball) while playing on the lawn of Cliefden House, in Buckinghamshire. An abcess formed internally and burst while he was dancing at Leicester House. So one of the game's greatest enthusiasts became its victim. The wonder, then as now, is that there were not many more victims to the rock-hard 'sporting' missile.

3. WILLES SHOWS THE WAY

Howard and Wells—death of 'Little Joey'—Squire
Osbaldeston—Brown of Brighton—John Willes
Lillywhite and Broadbridge—the roundarm revolution

As Hambledon's fame began to fade towards the end of the
eighteenth century, the Marylebone Cricket Club was
founded and Thomas Lord laid out the first of his three
grounds in 1787. By 1800 the pool of cricketing talent was
firmly established in the county of Surrey, though one of the
two fastest bowlers of the time was Tom Howard, born at
Hartley Wintney, a gamekeeper, father of nineteen children,
who was a genuine all-rounder in that he made runs, was
a fine single-wicket player, and was introduced to big cricket
by David Harris as a wicketkeeper. His career was long—
he played in the Gentlemen v Players match in 1829 when
aged 48—and as with all the rest, his achievements are
recorded more by word than statistic, since the bowler's
name did not appear on the scoresheet unless he bowled
his victim.

The other eminent fast bowler, also no youngster, at the
turn of the century was 'Honest John' Wells, a baker and
brother-in-law of Billy Beldham, with whom he once shared
the extraordinary tribute of a pub sign in their native village
of Wrecclesham which read 'The Rendezvous of the celebrated Cricketers Beldham and Wells'.

Probably the first major casualty of the 1800s occurred in
1800, when John 'Little Joey' Ring, who habitually stepped in
front of his wicket to play balls to leg, was smashed on the

nose by a kicker from his brother George. He was laid up for several weeks, but after a temporary recovery he died. The gods may have taken him in the name of lbw, for his placing of his legs in front of the stumps (Tom Taylor was the other arch culprit of the times) branded him as justification personified for the new Law, established in 1774, against such 'shabby' practice. Sir Horace Mann, another of the game's great patrons, employed the Ring brothers on his estate at Bourne House, near Canterbury, John the elder as whipper-in and George as huntsman. John's bat, inscribed 'Little Joey', survives at Lord's.

After Harris, bowling standards declined, and the advance in batting technique was continued by amateurs such as William Ward, E. H. Budd, George Osbaldeston, and the Reverend Lord Frederick Beauclerk, and by a proliferation of professionals, William Lambert the champion of them all. Batting averages rose steadily during the Napoleonic years. It was bound to bring a major riposte from the practitioners of the noble but unsung art of bowling.

There was still much drama and excitement in those seasons—and an alarming amount of 'fixing' and double-dealing. Heavy betting, especially on single-wicket matches, attracted some shady characters to Lord's and other centres, and the martyr, even if his hands were tainted, became no less a man than Lambert himself, who was banned at Lord's after allegedly 'selling' England's match against Nottingham.

Lambert made his name when the wicket was smaller and all bowling was underarm, but there can be no doubting his great talent. An attacking batsman, he stood with his bat over his shoulder, and specialised in the drive. In 1817 he became the first to score two centuries in a match, 107 not out and 157, at the present Lord's ground, for Sussex against Epsom, who included Budd and Tom Howard. Another century was scored for Sussex in that match: by Squire George Osbaldeston, who as an all-round sportsman and womaniser deserved—and wrote—an entire book on his life.

In 1810 Osbaldeston, a fast enough bowler to warrant two

long-stops, played with Lambert in a famous single-wicket match against Beauclerk and Tom Howard. It began under the shadow of the Squire's indisposition and Beauclerk's refusal to postpone the match. Lambert assured his partner that he could beat the other pair single-handed, so the match proceeded, with Osbaldeston managing one run before he retired ill, which allowed the taking of a substitute. Lambert then made 56 and 24, and dismissed Beauclerk and Howard twice apiece, His Lordship being outwitted the second time when Lambert purposefully bowled wide for some little while (there was no penalty then for a wide ball). Beauclerk lost his temper, got out, and Lambert carried off the stakes.

A further instance of frayed temper accounted for the exit from the big-time of Osbaldeston himself. In 1818 he was matched against George Brown, from Brighton, a devastating bowler who once at practice bowled a ball clean through a coat held tremblingly by long-stop and up against presumably the skull of a loitering dog, which died instantly. Another of Brown's long-stops, Dench by name, felt safe only with a sack of straw tied to his chest. Brown beat Osbaldeston comprehensively, and the furious Squire went straight to the members' list at Lord's and scratched his name from it. Later he repented, but Lord Frederick Beauclerk would not allow his re-entry.

Edward Hayward Budd, using a 3 lb bat in an era when underarm bowling demanded as heavy an instrument as was consistent with comfort, was a powerful batsman against whom the bowlers could truly measure themselves. He and William Ward and others of almost equal ability with the bat during the first twenty years of the nineteenth century exposed underarm bowling for the largely ineffective and outmoded form of attack that it was. Ward, Member of Parliament, director of the Bank of England, saviour (through his chequebook in a time of crisis) of Lord's Cricket Ground, astonished the sporting world by scoring 278 for MCC against Norfolk in 1820, a ground record for 105 years.

Another eye-popping score was registered in 1826 by the first of Yorkshire's champions, Tom Marsden. For Sheffield

& Leicester he made 227 against Nottingham (with William Clarke and Thomas Barker, no less), at Sheffield's Darnall ground—and he was only 22. A left-handed all-rounder, he was also capable of bowling a very brisk underarm, and was an ideal single-wicket competitor. Often all his fieldsmen were placed behind the wicket, so fierce was his pace. He played two contests against Fuller Pilch, losing both; but the match at his home ground in Sheffield—a three-day affair—drew a crowd of 20,000. Alas, he seems to have burned himself out by the age of 25; but he did much to put Northern cricket on the map.

The scene was now set for John Willes, from Kent, an all-round sportsman, to inspire a change of the profoundest significance in conduct, character and Law.

It is said that Willes first saw the possibilities of round-arm (i.e. bowling with the arm horizontal or slightly below) in his sister Christina's action: she was prevented by her hooped skirts from bowling underarm. In 1807, on Penenden Heath, playing for Twenty-three of Kent against Thirteen of England, he bowled roundarm, and the *Morning Herald* reported that this 'new' form of attack 'proved a great obstacle against getting runs in comparison to what might have been got by straightforward bowling'. The word 'straightforward' was really pregnant with meaning.

The wretched Willes became increasingly unpopular in the fifteen years that followed, and was barred in some quarters, jeered in others when he did perpetrate his illegal form of attack. But others emulated him, notably William Ashby, a carpenter, like Willes a resident of Sutton Valence. E. H. Budd and William Lambert tried it, with success, until the mighty William Ward denounced it—because, it was suggested, he was powerless against it.

The climax came on July 15, 1822, at Lord's. Opening the bowling for Kent against an MCC side which included Beauclerk, Ward, Budd and the club's secretary Benjamin Aislabie, Willes was no-balled by umpire Harry Bentley (some reports attribute the action to his colleague, Noah Mann, son of the Hambledon player who died after falling

29

into a fireplace during the night). The aggrieved bowler hurled the ball to the ground in disgust, walked to his horse, and rode away, never again to appear in a match of any consequence. He died in 1852 at the age of 74, 'in fearfully reduced circumstances', and it was some years before, through the consideration of friends, a memorial was erected over his final resting place.

In contrast, a fine monument was to be erected by the noblemen and gentlemen of the Marylebone Club over the grave of F. W. (William) Lillywhite, who died two years after Willes, having carried the roundarm cause to fulfilment.

Lillywhite was born near Goodwood on June 13, 1792, and became a bricklayer under his father, who managed two large brickyards owned by the Duke of Richmond. In 1822 he moved to Brighton, from which point his career flourished, albeit later in life than is usual. He stood only 5 ft 4 ins, and bowled a slow but exceptionally accurate ball, and although no great runmaker, he showed courage, once facing 278 balls from the terrifying George Brown while wearing no gloves.

In 1837 he became landlord of the Royal Sovereign, in Brighton, and proprietor of a cricket ground, but by 1844 he had run into business difficulties, and at the age of 52 he started a new life in London, becoming engaged as a ground bowler by MCC. But his imperishable mark on cricket history was made in 1827, when 'the Nonpareil bowler', as he was universally known, with his collaborator in the new style of bowling, James Broadbridge, a fast-medium bowler and bachelor farmer from Duncton, Sussex, played in a series of three experimental matches, Sussex v All England, to assess the wisdom or otherwise of legalising roundarm bowling.

Sussex won the first, at Sheffield, by seven wickets, and the second, at Lords, by three wickets—with Ward (42 and 20) the only batsman to master the new-style attack. At this point the professionals in the England side refused to play the third match 'unless the Sussex players bowl fair, i.e. abstain from throwing', but a reorganisation of the England team enabled the match to be played, and Sussex were this time defeated by 24 runs. The reversal probably pleased William Lillywhite, in his tall hat and cotton braces, and Jem Broadbridge, for it was partly engineered by George Thomas Knight, a nephew of Jane Austen, who himself employed roundarm—now referred to as 'the March of Intellect' style of bowling. The bickering and controversy reached new heights, but the revolutionaries now had in Knight a capable, fluent advocate. He pursued the cause through a series of letters to the *Sporting Magazine*, stating that batting's dominance over bowling had become detrimental to cricket and that proposals to increase the size of the wicket would only reduce the science of the game. References to the new style as 'throwing' were nonsense: a straight arm was the antithesis of a throw.

Resistance was headed by player/journalist William Denison, who feared the effect of the increased pace on hard pitches, by William Ward, by die-hard Thomas Lord, and by John Nyren, who expressed the fear that 'the elegant and scientific game of cricket will degenerate into a mere exhibition of rough, coarse horseplay!'

At its spring meeting in 1828 MCC modified Rule 10 to permit the bowler's hand to be raised as high as the elbow, with the back of the hand uppermost if required, but little effect was felt, and Lillywhite and Broadbridge continued to bowl from shoulder-height, and the umpires did nothing to stop them. The method spread rapidly, and inevitably MCC legalised pure roundarm bowling in 1835. The Law read: 'The Ball must be bowled, and if it be thrown or jerked, or if the hand be above the shoulder in the delivery, the umpire must call "No Ball".'

Bowlers, as ever, wanted more. The arm often passed higher than the shoulder, and it took the phenomenon of Alfred Mynn's express bowling to persuade MCC in 1845 to strengthen the Law so that no bowler would have the benefit of the doubt in the matter of the arm's height at the point of delivery.

Meanwhile, the art of batsmanship responded to the new challenge by raising its standards perceptibly, attaining a fresh sophistication.

4. MANLY MYNN AND 'FOGHORN'

Sam Redgate—Alfred Mynn—William Hillyer
Mynn escapes amputation—'Wacky' Kirwan
Walter Marcon—Harvey Fellows—John Wisden
John Jackson—'Tear 'em' Tarrant—Billy Buttress

The 'March of Intellect' had stormed the Winter Palace, as
it were, and a stability from the new order was awaited.
Instead, new bowlers grew up and bowled the newly-
allotted style at a pace foreseen by few. Batting improved,
possibly because it had to improve, and the old'uns shook
their heads and yearned for the days of yore.

Two outstanding fast bowlers came to notice. One was
Sam Redgate, a Nottingham professional, who won his success with speed and spin together with clever change of
pace. On this first appearance at Lord's assisting the
Gentlemen, he clean bowled the redoubtable Fuller Pilch
twice for nought, and four years later he bowled a celebrated over in shaving Pilch's wicket with the first ball,
bowling him with the second, bowling Mynn with the third,
and bowling Stearman with the fourth. At each success he
drank a glass of brandy, according to the cricket historian
James Pycroft, but if he was to leave the game at 36 and
die a broken man at 40 he had tasted glory reserved for few.

The other great figure, literally and metaphorically, was
Alfred Mynn, 'the Lion of Kent', eighteen stone at his
lightest, as generous a sportsman as ever swung an arm.
Born at Goudhurst, Kent, in 1807 in a line of large-bodied
yeomen, he was probably as old as eighteen when he first

33

played cricket. He was coached by none other than John Willes, who made a roundarm bowler of him. He was wildly erratic at first, and took an enormous run, but forsaking a little pace, he grew to become still fast and mercilessly accurate. That telegraph-pole arm would sweep round from his ox-like shoulder after only six majestic approach steps and the ball would flash down on the line of the leg stump and whip across to hit the off.

Batting against Mynn and those of almost equal ferocity could be a dangerous business. Almost all bowlers operated from around the wicket before the introduction of overarm bowling, and this alone beset the batsman with an awkward approach line. To be dismissed 'hat knocked on wicket' was not an unknown indignity. Batting technique was based on the drive and the cut, interspersed with the peculiar draw shot (between legs and wicket) and the dog-shot (ball stroked away under a raised front leg). The hook and pull shots were considered uncouth, and were rarely seen. On rough and very rough pitches a batsman's problems when faced by such as Alfred Mynn can easily be imagined. A tribute published in the *Sporting Life* after his death in 1861 assists the vision :

> *How perfectly grand was the advance of Mr Mynn to the wicket to deliver the ball—the very earth seemed to tremble under his measured, manly, and weighty stride, as, with form upright, his vast chest expanded, 'thud' would come down the left foot on the sward, the right arm would shoot out, and, with a majestic sweep, round, low, and as fair as law X itself, away shot the ball, as if propelled from a Whitworth gun, and, if straight, woe to the unlucky wicket opposite.*

Woe also to an unfortunate second long-stop who once took a ball from Mynn in the chest and spat blood for a fortnight.

Never satisfactorily explained was Mynn's ability to make the ball hum through the air. It may have been from the cut or spin he put on the ball (Arthur Mailey, Australia's leg-spinner of the 1920s, could 'drag a tune' out of the ball), or it may have been from a raised seam. Fast bowlers throughout the ages have frequently weakened to the temptation to alter the shape and balance of the ball—all that's needed is a strong thumbnail! Whether Mynn, an honourable man (did he not threaten to knock down a baronet who approached him, knowing of his recurring penury, with a 'foul proposal', i.e. to sell a match?), would resort to such a sneaky practice will never be known for certain.

Mynn was also a superb batsman and a short slip whose capacious hands missed very little. For twenty years he was a pillar of the Gentlemen's XI, and one of the most renowned and popular figures in England. He was part of a mighty Kent XI who filled the grounds from early morning till the last ball—usually triumphant to Kent—was bowled, an eleven of whom W. J. Prowse truly wrote: 'And with five such mighty cricketers, 'twas but natural to win, As Felix, Wenman, Hillyer, Fuller Pilch, and Alfred Mynn.'

Felix was Nicholas Wanostrocht, a small left-handed batsman who excelled in the cut, perhaps the Neil Harvey of his day, except that he was slow between wickets. He was a versatile man, a schoolteacher by profession, a fine watercolour artist, inventor of the Catapulta, an automatic bowling machine, and tubular india-rubber batting gloves. Edward Gower Wenman was a good batsman but famed for his wicketkeeping. A large man, born and bred in the village of Benenden, 'Ned' had a long career, and spent much of it keeping wickets to Mynn's thunderous bowling. As an off-shoot to classic fast bowling there has always been the opportunity it affords for wicketkeepers to demonstrate their skill, and Wenman, truly ambidextrous, built his reputation largely from his taking of Mynn's deliveries. Herbert Jenner, another Kent player and the outstanding University player of his day, also excited much admiration for his clean handling of Mynn's peerless bowling—and without the comforts of gloves or pads. Such protection came gradually into vogue as the fast roundarm men inflicted their painful impressions on thumb and thigh, chin and shin, over the years.

Of Mynn's other main comrades-in-arms, William Hillyer was his chief bowling ally, possessing a beautiful action and making the ball lift sharply and move unpleasantly from leg to off. His pace was brisk, though he was not a pronouncedly fast bowler, the proof being that he was chosen to play for the fast bowlers against the slow in 1840 and for the slow against the fast two years later though his pace had not diminished in the meantime. His reliable catching at short slip was of great assistance to Mynn.

Finally, there was Fuller Pilch, Norfolk-born but a wanderer, now landlord of the Saracen's Head at Canterbury, and the pride of Kent. For years he was the finest batsman in England—and therefore the world—playing upright and generally forward in a most commanding manner. He made at least ten centuries, which in the context of the period was a stupendous performance, comparable perhaps with someone today registering ten scores of 250 or more in a career.

These men, with their nearer-life-size contemporaries, brought glory to Kent. Of opposing bowlers there were, of course, many of considerable pace and ability, young Sir Frederick Bathurst (seen by James Pycroft in later years with his watch-chain plumbing a perpendicular almost clear of his toes) and Francis Fenner, who opened Fenner's ground at Cambridge, being two who caused batsmen constant anxiety. But Mynn, always Mynn, took what passed as headlines in the local newspapers of the day. Only two batsmen ever really showed signs of mastering him with any consistency: William Ward, who prepared himself by having professionals bowl at him from nineteen yards, and the Hon. Robert Grimston, who always took two bats to the crease, the heavier for dealing with Mynn. He delighted in driving him to the far reaches, where no fieldsman patrolled, since most were behind the wicket for Mynn and any other express bowlers. Mynn had to run and chase for himself, but usually saw the humorous side, as he did when Grimston confided that he called his bat 'Mynn's master'.

In 1836 Alfred Mynn's career was almost ended by injury. Fresh from a grand all-round triumph for MCC against Sussex at Brighton (45 and 92, with nine wickets—seven bowled), he turned out for the South against the North before a huge gathering at Leicester. Before the match began, while practising, Mynn was struck on the right ankle by one of the Leicestershire professionals. Soon the ankle began to swell, and he had to have it bound up, reluctantly returning for the day to the Anchor Inn. He went in the following day at the fall of the eighth wicket, with a runner, and scrambled a useful 21 not out. Still in pain, he bowled hardly at all in the North's innings, which, thanks to Lilly-white's bowling, finished 55 runs short of the South's 165.

Mynn's leg, by the third day, had swollen alarmingly, and a normal being would have withdrawn from the match. But he limped out to bat at the fall of the third wicket and, in constant agony, hit the bowling all over the field. Red-gate was at his best, bowling at a stupendous rate, but 'the better I bowled, the harder he hit me away!' Many times, according to the law of averages, Mynn was hit by Redgate, and the leg took a terrible battering during his five-hour innings. But he finished with 125 not out, taking his aggregate to an incredible 283 runs in two matches for twice out, and the sportswriters could think of no praise worthy enough. Now for the price.

Lord Frederick Beauclerk met him as he approached the tent, and escorted him inside. There a fearful sight met their eyes as Mynn removed his trousers. The leg, usually the size of Goliath's, was grotesque from swelling and inflammation. It was unbelievable that a man could have stood on it, let alone batted—and against Redgate—for five hours. Beauclerk instructed him immediately to journey home and find the best medical attention available. Mynn awaited the next Leicester-to-London stagecoach.

The next problem was to place him inside the vehicle. When this was found to be impossible he was hoisted onto the roof, secured as safely as possible, and thus began a new kind of agony for him as he was conveyed a hundred miles over imperfect roads. By the time he reached London there was no question of his being transported to Kent, and he was put up at the Angels Tavern in St Martins Lane. For some time surgeons were doubtful that they could save the leg, and even his continued existence was open to question. Felix later recounted that an amputation was imminent when Mynn, a religious man, asked for five minutes alone to pray. During those fateful minutes the surgeons, who apparently had decided that the leg should be removed at the hip joint, reconsidered.

Mynn spent some time in St Bartholomew's Hospital, and recovered slowly. He might have returned to cricket the following year, 1837, except that his parents died within three months of each other. This was to alter drastically the circumstances of Alfred and his brother Walter, for their father had supported them staunchly, and enabled them to play freely—as amateurs. Cricket—like real life—is pitted with ironies, and to add to that of the great fast bowler's grievous injury from fast bowling was that his first-born, a son, died two hours after birth in December 1837, and a second son died in 1843 after six weeks on this earth. Five children were to live—and, though their great manly father loved them dearly, all were girls.

He returned to the game in 1838, sometimes wearing protection around the leg, and for a season or two feeling the after-effects. But for the rest of his career he bestrode the scene like a favourite monarch, frequently carrying the Gentlemen to victory over the Players in those all-important matches, and earning for himself the title of Champion of England by his indomitable single-wicket play. In 1838, at Town Malling, Kent, Mynn, resplendent in red-ribboned straw hat, comprehensively beat the little Yorkshireman, James Dearman, and repeated the exercise a week later on Dearman's home ground. Each time, thousands turned up, and were left in little doubt that Mynn was the country's outstanding cricketer. It was eight years before he was challenged again, this time by Felix, as unlikely a 'David' as any, for he was a 'touch' batsman whose bowling was comparatively innocent. He hoped to have Mynn caught from his slow bowling, but with no runs permitted from strokes backward of square either side of the wicket, Felix resisted 518 balls in two matches but scored only four runs from his bat. Large crowds, with galaxies of celebrities (including John Willes, Mynn's early mentor), watched the historic contests, at Lord's and Bromley, most probably aware that their eyes beheld the greatest single-wicket player to date. There can have been very few equipped to beat him from that day to this.

Understandably, once he passed forty his bowling waned, though he made runs—in his usual robust manner. His weight burgeoned to twenty-three or twenty-four stone, well beyond W. G. Grace's bulk and edging out even 'the Big Ship', Warwick Armstrong. One wonders to what extent their very size gave these champions a psychological edge over their adversaries. Mynn's misfortunes extended to bankruptcy and several spells in debtors' prison, his financial embarrassment being eased by a successful testimonial at Lord's in 1847. There, for Kent against England, he made top score in the match, 48, bowled as fast as ever to take nine wickets, and made the winning hit.

During the 1850s age caught up with the great Kent XI. No longer could they hold their own against All-England; no longer could they depend upon full houses. New players were needed, but complete transfusions take time. One of the most promising was a fast left-hander from Benenden, Edmund Hinkly, who raised eyebrows at Lord's by taking six England wickets in the first innings, and all ten (five bowled) in the second, this with Mynn and Hillyer also bowling. But Hinkly's health let him down, and his career was destined to be brief though brilliant. Another was Edgar Willsher, a fastish left-arm bowler who began playing in good company while still in his teens. When, in 1851, he took the wickets of Joseph Guy, William Caffyn, and George Parr when playing for Kent against England, the sages grudgingly acknowledged that a new star was in the making, the only reservation being that Willsher's arm

39

tended to stray above shoulder-level. Like John Willes before him, Edgar Willsher was to become the centre of a storm of controversy whose passing was to leave cricket a profoundly changed game.

Meanwhile, roundarm bowling in the 1840s had reached such a pace and proficiency that—in big matches at least—runs really had to be earned. Not that all bowlers yet raised their arms to the level permitted since 1835. J. H. 'Wacky' Kirwan bowled jerkily with a low arm, but at a very fast pace, once knocking a bail thirty yards, and in 1835, for Eton, bowling all ten wickets down in MCC's second innings. A year later he bowled out fifteen batsmen for the Undergraduates against Cambridge Town, at Parker's Piece. The scorecard would make attractive wallpaper, blistered as it is with 'b J. H. Kirwan' again and again. The Church's gain was cricket's loss when he took up an appointment as curate of St Feock, Cornwall.

Eton produced two more tearaways in 1841 and 1842, during which years Harvey Fellows and Walter Marcon appeared in the eleven. Marcon's bowling warranted three long-stops and a wicketkeeper standing well back. In his two matches against Harrow he took fourteen wickets, thirteen of them clean bowled, and at Oxford he broke a batsman's leg. He and Fellows (who, like Mynn, could make the ball hum like a top) let the ball go from an angle roughly midway between underarm and roundarm.

W. G. Grace, in his book *Cricket* (1891), wrote of Marcon's bowling against the West Gloucestershire Club in 1846 (two years before WG was born): 'Their wickets went down like ninepins, and half of the batsmen never saw the ball when he bowled. Every fieldsman was behind the wicket, and there were two long-stops: the first stood fifteen yards behind, and was supposed to be the wicketkeeper; and the second about thirty yards farther away. Mr Marcon did not trouble about the length of the ball. He aimed at the wicket, and the ball flew straight from his hand to it without touching the ground; and nearly every time it hit the bottom of the stump, the stump was smashed.

Runs were scored now and then from a snick to leg or slip, but not one of them could hit him in front of the wicket. A member of the team said it could be done— ought to be done, and *he* would do it!' (This might almost have been drawn from England's plight in the 1974–75 series against Australia, with Tony Greig attempting to grasp the initiative.) '"It is no use grounding your bat and waiting until he bowls," said he. "No! have your bat in the air in hitting position, and let fly at him." He was certainly big enough and strong enough to do as he said; so in he went, and stood waiting with the bat in the air, ready to hit. Mr Marcon came with a rush, and our enterprising member hit. The ball hit the bat high up about the shoulder, and bat and ball went right through the wicket.'

Henry Grace had firm ideas about Marcon: 'I can assure you that, while standing at point, I could hardly trace the ball.'

E. H. Budd, who played against both, said that the dreaded George Brown (who killed the dog) 'was not more terrific in his speed than Marcon'. Here the Church claimed another fast bowler, for Marcon abandoned the game after a few seasons, having played for Oxford University in 1843–44, eventually to become Rector of Edgefield, Norfolk. One other spectacular performance remains ensconced in the record books: he bowled four batsmen with consecutive balls for Attleborough against Swaffham in 1850. From these deeds and the written tributes of those who saw him we must accept, or otherwise, that Marcon was one of the fastest bowlers of all time, allowing that exceptional speed underarm can be as much of a surprise to the batsmen as exceptional speed overarm, even though the speediest of the former kind could hardly expect to touch the velocity of the best of the latter.

As for Marcon's colleague at Eton, Harvey Fellows, he once sent a stump flying into long-stop's hands eleven yards behind the wicket. Hertfordshire-born, Fellows liked to keep wicket occasionally, and was a big-hitter with the bat. But his fame rests on bowling so fast that in a Gentlemen *v*

Players match at Lord's he had the great Fuller Pilch playing him with his head half turned away. George Parr said he was the only bowler he could not punish with his famous hit to leg, and Tom Box, the Sussex wicketkeeper, declared that on rough ground no man in the world could play Fellows. His peak was also quickly reached and put behind him. Some attributed it to the raising of his arm action, which they thought cost him both speed and accuracy. Whatever the cause, it was time for batsmen to emit sighs of relief. Among his greatest achievements was to bowl down the first nine Gentlemen of Warwickshire's wickets and catch the tenth for 1 Zingari at Leamington. He and Nash bowled unchanged through both innings of Gentlemen of Kent for Gentlemen of England at Lord's, while at Canterbury in 1864, when aged 38, he dismissed G. M. Kelson so comprehensively that not one of the three stumps remained in the ground. He lived on till 80, serving on the MCC committee and as the club's legal advisor, and for decades listening to fellow members compare the speed of any new lights with his own.

One of the most remarkable statistics in cricket's annals is the ten wickets, all bowled, taken by John Wisden for North against South at Lord's in 1850. A pop-eyed little man of only 5 ft 4 ins and weighing, at the start of his career, seven stone (less than the diminutive leg-spinner of the 'twenties and 'thirties, Tich Freeman!), Wisden filled out to eleven stone as the seasons passed. He had a beautiful movement, and came through from his roundarm action at a great pace, made all the more surprising by his slight stature. Allied to this was a huge break from the off, and it is said that his famous 'all-ten' were *clean-bowled*, i.e. bowled without any of the batsmen even getting a touch with pad or bat. His name lives with *Wisden Cricketers' Almanack*, still the student's premier source of reference in spite of countless challengers over the years, though the annual's growth could hardly have been anticipated in 1863 when the 37-year-old founder, his fast-bowling days behind him, put together the inaugural, 112-page issue. Today the Almanack takes up $2\frac{1}{4}$ ins of shelf space, and records the deeds of thousands of cricketers—men of pace and men of peace alike.

Two important Surrey players during the 1850s and 1860s were Tom Sherman, a very fast roundarm bowler who had that something extra which proclaimed the occasional delivery from him as 'unplayable', and Heathfield Harman Stephenson, who bowled fast-medium off-breaks that owed much to his curious right thumb, which he could put out of joint at will. Both became public school coaches, Stephenson turning into a legend at Uppingham and Sherman, who lived to be 83, passing on his knowledge at Harrow, Eton, Winchester, and Rugby. It is often said that bowlers make the best coaches.

Stephenson seems to have gone into decline as a bowler because of overbowling. Undeterred, he concentrated on his batting and wicketkeeping, and kept an eye on his nephew, Maurice Read, also of Thames Ditton, who went on to play for Surrey and England. Stephenson's greatest claim to fame is that he led the first English tour to Australia, in 1861–62, winning much praise for his dignified captaincy.

As Kent's great days fell behind them, Nottinghamshire and Surrey emerged as the strongest counties, Nottinghamshire having a strong array of bowlers. James Grundy, a fast-medium bowler, was engaged by MCC for 21 seasons, and played also for the Players and William Clarke's All-England XI; yet he missed only one important match for his county between 1851 and 1867. He was a 'dream' partner for any fast bowler in that he preferred bowling into the wind! Even-tempered, steady in length and direction (leg stump), his only complaint seems to have been that at Brighton 'the ball don't get half-stump high'—a grievance his descendants of the 1970s in county cricket would echo loudly of many pitches upon which they have to bowl.

John Bickley served Nottinghamshire as a fast roundarm bowler in the early 1850s and saw more glory than most who have played twice as long. In 1853, at Lord's, he bowled Nottinghamshire to unforeseen victory when England needed only 76 to win: in forty four-ball overs he took 8 for 23. In the next match, against Sussex, he took 4 for 28 and 6 for 16, and against Surrey he took 9 for 54. He took an engagement with the Earl of Stamford, and was an irregular player at 'first-class' level, though he continued to turn in startling figures, as for instance his 8 for 7 for England against Kent & Sussex at Lord's in 1856. Originally a jumper and walker of some eminence, Bickley had an easy approach to the crease and a lovely free action. His pace off the pitch was said never to have been equalled until the advent of the great Yorkshireman, George Freeman.

There was a need in Nottinghamshire, the county of Clarke and Parr and Guy and Tinley and, soon, Richard Daft, for someone with that extra edge of speed. He arrived in 1855: just over 6 ft and weighing fourteen stone, John Jackson, very fast, though his approach was only three or four yards, very straight, the type to set a batsman's cheeks flushing, especially on a damp or uneven wicket. He was born in Bungay, Suffolk, but was taken to Wellow, a village in Nottinghamshire, when only a week old. William Clarke spotted his potential when he played matches in the early 1850s against Clarke's travelling All-England XI, and he made his debut for Nottinghamshire (on Clarke's Trent Bridge ground) in August, 1855.

There was no looking back. During his peak seasons, 1857 to 1863, he took 671 wickets in important matches at around ten runs apiece, and only one century was scored (by William Caffyn) against his side in all that time. Caffyn, when he thought of Jackson in later years, recalled his habit of bowling an occasional full-toss towards the head (a 'beamer' in modern parlance).

He was celebrated in verse—Prowse's 'Jackson's pace is very fearful' lives on—some of it a trifle macabre, and he became the first cricketer to be the subject of a *Punch* cartoon (August 29, 1863), a bystander saying to a battered batsman: 'Good match, old fellow?' 'Oh yes; awfully jolly!' 'What did you do?' 'I 'ad a hover of Jackson; the first ball 'it me on the 'and, the second 'ad me on the knee;

the third was in my eye; and the fourth bowled me out!'

Jackson, who developed into a hard-hitting batsman, toured America with the first English overseas team in 1859, and went—again under George Parr's leadership—to Australia in 1863–64. He returned some amazing analyses, including 10 for 10 against Twenty-two of United States at Hoboken, and 14 for 35 in the match against Twenty-two of New South Wales at Sydney. At home he made almost a habit of taking six, seven, eight, even nine wickets in an innings, the most pleasurable to him being his nine for North against South at Trent Bridge when he also incapacitated the remaining batsman, John Wisden. Even allowing that matches played by the All-England XI were against local Twenty-twos, his figures, to put it baldly, were impressive: 359 wickets in 1858, 346 in 1859, 331 in 1857.

He was nicknamed 'The Demon' and also 'Foghorn' for his habit of blowing his nose after taking a wicket, and to judge from his bowling figures he must have got through some handkerchiefs in a season. At Uppingham he once bowled six men in seven balls, and at Truro he took eight wickets in sixteen balls. At Cranbrook, in 1863, he took thirteen wickets in the match, held four catches, and scored 100 runs to beat Kent practically single-handed.

His effectiveness was reduced from 1866, when he ruptured a blood vessel in his leg while chasing a ball at Trent Bridge, and for several years to come he was engaged here and there as a professional. But in its entirety his is one of the most tragic of cricket lives, for the young lad who ran barefoot after hounds grew to a great manliness only to subside into abject poverty, working, stooped and white-bearded, as a warehouseman in Liverpool and then eking out an existence on six shillings a week from the Cricketers' Friendly Society and from the hospitality of acquaintances. Long-gone were the days when he collected his payment in gold sovereigns—the lot once falling through a torn pocket during his innings, Jackson loudly refusing the aid of other players to pick up the coins: 'Get out o' th' road and let me pick it oop mysen!' He died in the workhouse infirmary in 1901, aged 68, and was given a pauper's burial.

Across in Cambridgeshire another fast bowler, ranked for a time as second in speed to John Jackson, was George Tarrant (born George Tarrant Wood). He was much smaller but hardly less destructive, bowling round the wicket, roundarm, from a long, lively run-up ('all over the place like a flash of lightning' wrote WG), often bowling a batsman off his legs. He was by every account not the most pleasant of men, and certainly could not stand to have runs taken from his bowling. In favourable conditions there seemed no obvious way of countering him at all, and one of the highlights of late-nineteeth-century cricket was to see Robert Carpenter, a complete master of back-play, enduring against the terrifying twin-pronged attack of Tarrant and Jackson.

Tarrant liked to play single-wicket, and was successful, sometimes, when touring, either home or abroad, taking on an entire eleven of the locals. Undistinguished batsman that he was, his frenzied action and dynamite delivery usually left him with little to do with the bat.

He died in 1870 at the early age of 31, and his Cambridgeshire bowling partner Billy Buttress lived only just beyond his fortieth birthday, having had 'a failing for pints'. Buttress was, so far as can be ascertained, a 'first'. He bowled medium-pace, but with a persistent and deadly leg-break, so much more difficult to initiate and control than the infinitely more common off-break, off-cutter, or, as it was known towards the end of last century, the breakback. Buttress claimed countless wickets from catches to slip and 'keeper, adding to them a great number of victims bowled round their legs by balls which seemed to be destined for widish of leg stump.

Tarrant may have had a high opinion of himself, but Buttress seems to have been a down-to-earth character. Certainly he was a hopeless batsman, and once when he was called to go in, he was found sitting in a tree: 'What's the good of me goin' in? If I miss 'em I'm out, and if I hit 'em I'm out. Let's start the next innings!'

Buttress was something of a ventriloquist, specialising in

a cat's mew, and even carried a stuffed kitten around with him, planting it in such unlikely places as under railway carriage seats. The 'cat's' hissing and swearing when elderly ladies sat over him caused many an uproar.

Buttress was as colourful a character as any fast bowler —and they have been a colourful lot.

5. OVERARM COMES TO STAY

Edgar Willsher—WG's influence—George Freeman
Tom Emmett—Hill and Ulyett—Jemmy Shaw
Fred Morley—Arthur Appleby—Martin McIntyre
Aborigines Mullagh, Marsh and Gilbert—Jack Crossland
Lang and Powys—death of George Summers

Someone was going to have to carry bowling through its
next transition, from roundarm to overarm—'above the
shoulder'. Someone was going to have to place this evolu-
tionary issue squarely before the authorities, compelling
them to clamp down on a spreading illegality. That someone
was Edgar Willsher, born at Rolvenden, in the Weald of
Kent, the youngest of a farmer's fourteen children, on
November 22, 1828. Tall, slim-faced and elegant, he was said
to have had only one lung since boyhood. Lord Harris, in
A Few Short Runs, recalled him as 'an attenuated, con-
sumptive-looking man' and that 'he had a curious faraway
look in his eyes, and used to look up at the sky as one talked
to him'. He played for Kent regularly for twenty-five years
from 1850, represented the Players for seventeen, and did
much to spread the fame of the roving All-England XI, bowling fastish left-arm with great accuracy, breaking sharply
from leg and getting maximum lift from any pitch.

Willsher was by no means the only man whose arm
seemed most of the time to be above the legal level, yet his
arm was the one chosen by umpire John Lillywhite (son of
the man who induced legislation to allow roundarm).

The date was August 27, 1862; place—The Oval; time—

evening, with Surrey's openers, Mortlock and Humphrey, about to reply to England's total of 503. Willsher, beginning his third over, walked quietly and quickly up to the crease as usual, delivered with his long, thin left arm, and was no-balled by Lillywhite at his end. To the next delivery there was another shout of 'no-ball', and to the next and the next and the next and the next. Understandably this was too much for the bowler, who strode from the field of play followed by his eight fellow professionals. Only V. E. Walker and C. G. Lyttelton, the England amateurs, stayed on the ground. The scene, as during the bomb scare during the 1973 Lord's Test, was one of bewilderment and spasmodic excitement. There was no further play that day, and after Street had taken Lillywhite's place as umpire next morning the game proceeded without further incident. Nonetheless, Lillywhite, who was a friend of Willsher's (the friendship was broken temporarily from this fateful day), had, by no-balling the best bowler in the land in one of the most important matches of the season, lain a contentious matter at the feet of the Marylebone Club.

Two years later, on June 10, 1864, Law 10 was rewritten, allowing bowlers to swing their arms through at any height, and Willsher found his place in history as more than a master practitioner of the art of bowling.

Unlike the martyr Willes, Willsher continued to play at major level for a decade afterwards, captaining an English side to America in 1868.

Curiously, his action had been thought by some to be within the pre-1864 legal definition. Richard Daft, the Nottinghamshire batting stylist, who considered him the best left-arm bowler he ever faced, felt that Willsher's arm *at the moment of delivery* was not above shoulder level. 'It cannot be denied', he explained in his book *A Cricketer's Yarns*, 'that to the spectators who did not watch him most closely he appeared to deliver above the shoulder. As a matter of fact, I believe that when the ball left his hand it was exactly on a level with his shoulder. He came up to the wicket with a quick-march kind of step; raised his hand high above his head, bringing it down, however, with a very quick jerky movement just as he delivered. That last movement of his seemed to put a spin and impetus on the ball that caused it to rise like lightning from the pitch. It seemed to reach one almost before it left his hand sometimes.'

Cricket, the twopenny weekly which ran from 1882 to 1913, recorded upon his death in 1885: 'Willsher often pathetically remarked that he had been born too soon: and, perhaps, to a certain extent he had cause to think so, for he lived to see "chuckers, half-chuckers, windmills, and pounding-down bowlers" have a good time of it, whilst he, a bowler with a strictly fair delivery, as regards bowling, had to be settled for occasionally delivering the ball above the shoulder.' Since the words emanated from Robert Thoms, the best-respected umpire of his time, they carry weight.

Daft, who employed back-play more profitably than forward-play to Willsher, accorded him the ultimate tribute in saying that he was the type of bowler a batsman—even one who was well set—was always glad to see taken out of the attack.

For the United South against Sixteen of Southgate in 1867 he bowled 27 overs of which 26 were maidens. Batsmen everywhere must have breathed more easily when 'Ted' Willsher eventually gave up playing and donned the umpire's coat.

The year 1864 was to see another important milestone for cricket: W. G. Grace, then only sixteen, attracted wide attention with innings of 170 and 56 not out in a match at Brighton. 'WG' was to become monarch of the game, a colossus whose performances, chiefly with the bat, clearly outstripped all others, a huge, bearded man, famous throughout Britain for decade after decade, who did more than any other mortal and as much as the fanning out of the railways, which took the game to the people, to make cricket a national pursuit and fascination.

During the 1870s, 1880s and 1890s his was the wicket above all others that bowlers prized; against him a bowler could truly say he was measuring his skill. It was said often, and verified, that WG 'killed professional fast bowling', that the fast men, even on sub-standard pitches, were hit away so monotonously—and their 'shooters' were stopped so surely—that they were satisfied to bowl a good 'width' to the Gloucestershire doctor. Batsmen were inspired by him, and bowlers were once again forced to think deeply about their methods. By the mid-1870s straight-out fast bowling was already in decline, and a generation of medium-pace bowlers was hatching.

WG drove and cut, played forward and back with equal ease, and lifted batting to an undreamt-of plane. Consequently much honour attaches to the name of the fast bowler W. G. Grace considered the best he played against. This was George Freeman, of Yorkshire. He was born at Boroughbridge on July 28, 1844, stood 5 ft 10½ ins and weighed an impressive fourteen stone. 'When the ball hit you,' WG wrote in his book *Cricket*, 'you felt as if you had been cut with a knife or a piece of the skin had been snipped off.'

Freeman, a kindly-faced auctioneer, had an easy action just above roundarm, could bowl long spells, and spun the ball mainly from the off. He also generated brisk pace off the pitch, in the manner of Tate and Hammond and Bedser in years to come, and was distinctly faster than he appeared from anywhere other than the striker's wicket.

He first confronted WG at Sheffield in 1869, for North v South, and the 21-year-old master made 122. In the second innings Freeman bowled him with a shooter, and WG remembered over twenty years later how the ball continued to spin for a few seconds at the base of the stumps.

The Yorkshireman played only 26 county matches before business lured him away, but in those contests he took as many as 194 wickets (average 7½ per match) at less than ten runs each. His favourite ground was The Oval, where the near-perfect wickets, even in those days, allowed him to regulate the degree of turn, eliminating chance—or in blunter terms, fluke. There was a similarity here with the outlook of the finest of slow left-arm bowlers, Wilfred Rhodes, of Yorkshire and England, in that he delighted most of all in bowling to the king of hitters, Gilbert Jessop, and the prince of inventive stylists, Victor Trumper.

The fame of Freeman's comrade-in-arms, Tom Emmett, has been perpetuated because of two attributes: a left arm capable of bowling a cricket ball at speed with spin from leg, and a tongue which uttered a lifetime of sardonic quotes. He was born in Halifax on September 3, 1841, and stood only 5 ft 8 ins. As a youth he bowled roundarm and by the time overarm was legalised he, like a great many others, saw no good reason to change his style, which typically gave way to wides—only in Emmett's case of almost ridiculous frequency. Here he occupied a position of his own, just as William Martingell, the fast-bowling all-rounder of Surrey and Kent, was notorious in the 1840s for no-balling by overstepping the crease. When Emmett pitched on leg stump, however, the ball was often unplayable—he called it his 'sostenuter'—and W. G. Grace was as proud of a tall score against Emmett and Freeman as any other pair. Indeed, Freeman said of an innings of 66 by WG against them at Lord's in 1870: 'A more wonderful innings was never played. Tom Emmett and I have often said it was a marvel the doctor was not either maimed or unnerved for the rest of his days, or killed outright. I often think of his pluck on that day when I watch a modern batsman scared if a medium ball hits him on the hand. He should have seen our expresses flying about his ribs, shoulders and head.'

Emmett and Freeman were also capable batsmen. Emmett captained Yorkshire, successfully toured Australia and America, and was still a force when well into his forties. Among his more startling analyses were 16 for 38 against Cambridgeshire in 1869, 6 for 7 against Surrey in 1867 and 8 for 22 against the same county fourteen years later. George Pinder, Yorkshire's wicketkeeper, one of several who claimed or for whom it was claimed that they were the first to dispense with long-stop, described keeping to his fast bowlers as 'no joke'. Of Emmett he wrote: 'He used to "corkscrew" his deliveries in a very perplexing way. There was a certain ball which appeared going to leg, but which would whip in on the middle and off stumps. As soon as I saw that ball I gave the batsman up.'

Emmett was cricket coach at Rugby School in later years, and his shrewd and droll counsel were highly valued by the boys.

Yorkshire's continuing strength in fast bowling was ensured by the timely arrival of Allan Hill just as Freeman withdrew from the side. A hand-loom weaver, an easy-going man who was born in the village of Kirkheaton, which later gave the world the fabulous Hirst and Rhodes, Hill has the distinction of having played for England in the first two Test matches, both at Melbourne in 1876–77; moreover his record, limited though it may be, is a proud one: 101 runs at an average of 50.50 and six wickets for 130.

Tall, he had a shortish run-up and model action, and usually broke the ball from the off; but his main weapons were the time-honoured ones of good length and persistent straightness.

A contemporary was George Ulyett, who served Yorkshire gallantly for twenty years as an all-rounder—in fact as the backbone of the side. Large and enormously strong, 'Happy Jack' was at first a fast bowler whose prime asset was an ability to extract whatever lift there was in the wicket. He was good enough to take 7 for 36 for England against Australia at Lord's in 1884. Later, though, he became more of a batsman, registering numerous successes for county, country, the Players, and other representative elevens. Five times he toured Australia. In an era of sailing ships and stagecoaches that alone demanded uncommon stamina and resilience. He played in 23 Tests against Australia and two against South Africa. Against New South Wales at Sydney in 1879 he took four wickets with consecutive balls, though the match is better remembered for the riot which ended play on the Saturday, Ulyett being one of the players who muscularly protected their captain, Lord Harris, from the mob.

W. G. Grace may have held the Yorkshiremen Freeman and Emmett in the highest esteem, but the bowler he often bracketed with them was James Coupe Shaw, of Nottinghamshire (not to be confused with the great Alfred Shaw of the same county, who was a cunning and incredibly accurate medium-pacer). Jemmy Shaw was yet another left-arm fast bowler, with a high delivery. One of his assets was that, like Jeff Thomson today, he brought his bowling arm very quickly at the last moment from behind his body, making sighting difficult for the batsman. His duels with WG provided some of the best sports copy during the early 1870s. Twice within little more than a fortnight Shaw brought WG down for nought in the first innings only for the Champion to make a double-century in the second. Shaw's plaintive exclamation when under fire has been repeated often : 'It ain't a bit of use my bowling good 'uns to him now; it's a case of I puts the ball where I please and *he* puts it where he pleases.'

Some of Shaw's figures are almost indigestible : in 1867, in all matches, he took 450 wickets, but in 109 innings for his county he only once reached double-figures. He retired to his farm at the end of it all—one of the rare professional cricketers of those times to find real security.

Just as Shaw had filled the wide vacuum left in the Notts XI after John Jackson, so Fred Morley rose to eminence after Shaw's retirement and became probably the finest bowler in England for many seasons until 1883. Morley—who was succeeded in turn in the county ranks by Walter Wright, the first 'swerve' bowler of modern times, and Billy Barnes, neither of whom had extreme pace—was very fast, left-handed, roundarm, and could turn the ball either way, with the fast leg-break naturally the more deadly. Born on December 16, 1850, at Sutton-in-Ashfield, Morley was no more than 5 ft 9 ins tall, had an extraordinarily small head, and weighed only $10\frac{1}{2}$ stone. Yet he built up surprising pace, and in harness with the nagging, versatile Alfred Shaw, whether for Nottinghamshire, the Players, or for England against Australia, he presented a formidable problem for even the best batsmen. Usually attired in black-and-white striped shirt, Morley was a woeful batsman, and it was said that as he emerged from the Trent Bridge pavilion, bat in hand, the horse used to move instinctively between the shafts of the roller. He was an uncomplicated fellow, extremely popular, and no-one begrudged him his almost endless list of remarkable bowling figures, too extensive to incorporate here. No top batsman of the day ever ceased to respect his bowling, and their lesser brethren were just so much cannon fodder.

On Daft's 1879 tour of America Morley took 100 wickets at $3\frac{1}{2}$ each. 'If Morley bowled like a machine,' wrote Daft, 'he certainly resembled a machine that was well oiled and in perfect working order. Never have I seen a left-hand bowler with such a perfectly easy swing as poor Fred possessed.'

'Poor' Fred because on the voyage to Australia with the Hon. Ivo Bligh's 1882–83 English team he suffered a broken rib when their ship *Peshawur* was in collision with the barque *Glenroy* out of Colombo. He played two matches in Australia before the injury was recognised, and in great pain played one more game before being declared unfit for the rest of the tour. Back home in 1883, he played only in the match against Lancashire, and, a very sick man, despite the best medical attention obtainable, his condition worsened over the next eighteen months, and he died, much mourned, in his native village on September 28, 1884, of lung congestion, at the early age of 33.

It had already long been acknowledged that the team with a genuinely fast bowler had a head-start over opponents without such a spearhead, and the team with a pair of fast men started in a doubly advantageous position, though it was still to be many years before the custom of opening the attack with a fast bowler opposite a slow bowler was to give way to the invariable practice of mounting a twin-pronged blitzkreig. 'Bowlers win matches' is an ancient adage to which a corollary may be added: 'Fast bowlers win them more rapidly.' Further to that, *left-arm* fast bowlers, being in such profusion, were apparently as easily obtainable as their orthodox cousins.

Another of the 'cacky-handers' was Arthur Appleby, 6 ft and 13 stone, an amateur all-rounder from Lancashire whose special ability was to bring the ball 'with the arm' from outside the off stump, often bowling unwary batsmen who were allowing the ball to pass 'harmlessly' by. He was a complete joy to watch, taking a long run and bowling accurately without sign of tiring in even the longest stint. He played with distinction for the Gentlemen against the Players, taking 8 for 65 at Lord's on his debut, and toured North America in 1872 with R. A. Fitzgerald's all-amateur team, a tour recorded by the captain in one of the most amusing cricket books ever written, *Wickets in the West*, which tells of steady drinking, pleasant off-the-field company, and of Appleby's taking of wickets almost at will. He claimed never to have tried to 'work' the ball, from which it may be deduced that he was a 'natural', the ball deviating in flight and off the pitch simply because he was built the way he was and moved the way he did. He died in 1902, aged 59, of cancer of the liver, modest to the end and popular among both Lancastrians and cricket-lovers everywhere else.

Appleby's county contemporaries included Scottish-born Alec Watson, another tireless performer, who reduced his early pace then built it up again after batsmen took to advancing to the pitch of the ball. He bowled with fair regularity—to the distaste of all his opponents—a shooter! There was also William McIntyre, whose pace was distinctly brisk. They had the support, too, of Dick Pilling, a superb wicketkeeper who served the Red Rose county and England faithfully during the late 1870s and the 1880s, wearing the lightweight pads and flimsy gloves of the time. Like most of Lancashire's players then, he was born outside the county—in Bedfordshire—and like many cricketers who rose to fame he was destined to be cut down well short of old age. He died in 1891 aged only 35.

Elsewhere other fast bowlers, while not winning everlasting fame, had their moments of glory. George Howitt, who later played both for Nottinghamshire and Middlesex, dismissed W. G. Grace for a duck in each innings at Neath in 1868 when the Champion was playing for United South against Twenty-two of Cadoxton. Almost needless to say, Howitt, roundarm and breaking from leg, was a left-arm bowler. Then across the Atlantic was Charles Newhall, one of the great Philadelphia family of cricketers, whose pace was assessed as being up to George Freeman's. He bowled a consistent length and often kept the ball low, but his ability could truly be measured only against the infrequent visiting English teams. During one of these matches, in 1872, for Twenty-two of Philadelphia against the Gentlemen of England, he took 10 for 69 in the match and his partner, Meade, a left-hander, with whom he bowled unchanged through both innings, took 6 for 52. W. G. Grace, who played in the match, was full of praise for Newhall, as he was for C. K. Francis, of Rugby and the Gentlemen. Francis, who became a Metropolitan Police magistrate, was a fast roundarm bowler whose speciality was a bumper which most batsmen found nearly impossible to evade. In the Rugby v Marlborough school match at Lord's in 1869 he took seven wickets in the first innings and all ten in the second, and earned the distinction of selection for the Gentlemen against the Players at only 19. It would have been anything but a restful experience, either, to face Martin McIntyre of Nottinghamshire, brother of Lancashire's William. He bowled with an action variously described as 'cartwheel' and 'head-over-heels'—especially on a lively pitch, which, characteristically of the breed, brought out an extra fieriness in him. He bounced them, and interspersed, voluntarily or otherwise, a shooter, and struck fear into the hearts of all but the most resolute batsmen. With it all he would beam at his successes and at the discomforts he inflicted, yet express heartfelt concern at painful blows to the ribs, shins and knuckles. He was an unusually popular cricketer—a spiritual ancestor of Fred Trueman. He went with WG to Australia in 1873–74, and stayed out late more often than the captain considered good for him. One morning, anticipating the formidable WG's chastisement, McIntyre arrived at the ground in good time, smiling benignly, and called cheerily: 'Good morning, sir! McIntyre has just been talking to himself, and won't let it occur again.'

In 1868 the Australian Aborigines toured England, led by the old Surrey player Charles Lawrence, and providing a source of the deepest curiosity wherever they appeared. Rejoicing in such exotic names as Bullocky, Red Cap, Jim Crow, Tiger, Twopenny and Dick-a-Dick, they wore sashes of various colours to distinguish them in the field, and they played at such unexpected venues as Deer Park, Richmond, Blackburn, Bishop's Stortford, Turnham Green, Southsea, Reading, Witham and Rochdale, as well as at several of the major first-class grounds, including Lord's, where, needing 101 runs to beat MCC, they were put out for 45.

WG, though he did not play against them, considered them to be third-class by English standards, and certainly their attraction stemmed as much from their associated skills as from their cricket: they gave regular exhibitions of spear-throwing, boomerang-throwing (one went astray at Bootle and cut through a spectator's hat and lacerated his head), and Dick-a-Dick with his nulla-nulla provided a human target for a squad of ball-throwers, and was thought to have evaded or countered every single missile during the long and taxing tour.

The hero was Johnny Mullagh, a kind of early Sobers, who batted 'elegantly', sometimes kept wicket, and with his fastish bowling took 245 wickets at ten runs apiece. He shared the brunt of the bowling with Lawrence, who took 250 wickets at twelve, and the third-highest wicket-taker was Cuzens, who, apart from scoring nine fifties, took 114 wickets at 11.3. He was said to be a thoughtful bowler, very fast, with a higher arm than most, and one report stated that he was quicker than Lipscomb, the nippy Kent bowler.

Since that entertaining tour, with its pathetic undertone (most of the Aborigines disappeared into obscurity or died shortly afterwards, and one of them, King Cole, succumbed during the tour), surprisingly few Aborigines have made any impression on big cricket, and all have been fast bowlers. At the turn of the century Henry played for a time for Queensland and big Jack Marsh for New South Wales. In the 1930s Eddie Gilbert whistled them down for several seasons, inflicting on Don Bradman one of his fifteen ducks in first-class cricket; and in the 1960s Ian King briefly showed promise for Queensland. Marsh and Gilbert were the best of them and the most interesting, though Henry, when he was no-balled by umpire Cossart at Brisbane for throwing, gave cricket history one of its most hilarious quotes: 'You ——! You no-ball my good balls and the ones I did throw, you never. You know nothing about cricket!' The Englishmen who faced him during the 1903–04 tour thought him just about the fastest bowler they had ever seen, though his action seemed 'not above suspicion'.

Marsh, a highly likeable man who wore his blue New South Wales cap everywhere, even under his straw hat, was illiterate, but was still often observed in the tram 'reading' a newspaper which as often as not was upsidedown. He met the same fate as Henry, being no-balled for throwing during the 1900–01 season twice in Melbourne by Bob Crockett and *nineteen* times in Sydney by the same umpire. That was the end of him in first-class cricket.

Eddie Gilbert, a small wiry man, came from an Aboriginal settlement just outside Brisbane and had to be persuaded fairly vigorously to play in boots. He took a short run but harnessed astonishing power into the sweep of his bowling arm and the whippiness of his wrist. Some thought he threw—including umpire Barlow, who called him eleven times at Melbourne in 1931—but one thing was certain: for four or five overs he was *exceedingly* fast. He lacked stamina, he was black, and he came from the Cinderella State. Otherwise, he might have become Australia's first and so far only Aborigine Test player. David Forrest, in *That Barambah Mob*, a blend of fact and fancy, told of a batsman who carried to his grave a souvenir of Gilbert: '... nufactured in Austra ...' stamped in reverse on his head, the imprint from the ball after a blow by one of little Eddie's bumpers. 'When that ball hit the concrete she'd smoke!' recalled the narrator, picturing Gilbert's bowling on the concrete pitches of Brisbane's minor cricket.

Stan McCabe, who played three of cricket's greatest Test innings, considered a double-century made against Gilbert the best in all his career. The Brisbane pitch was under-prepared, and New South Wales found themselves 31 for three, with Kippax also in hospital after having his eyebrow opened by a bumper from Thurlow at which he had hooked too early after the fiery pace of Gilbert at the other end. Bradman, against the lithe black man who was bowling with such horrifying hostility, made 'the luckiest duck I ever made'. Out of such chaos imperishable batting deeds may —but so seldom do—arise.

The last word on Gilbert's bowling action comes from Bill Hunt, the New South Wales left-arm medium-pacer. In violent expression of his belief that the Aborigine, knowingly or not, 'chucked', Hunt deliberately threw a ball at him as he batted at his customary position of number eleven for Queensland. The umpires either did not notice or chose to take no action, Gilbert's stumps were wrecked, and as they walked off he put his arm round Hunt's shoulder and said, 'That was a plurry good ball, Bill.' Picturing it vividly years later, Hunt said with a broad grin : 'So you see, the little bugger couldn't tell a bowl from a chuck anyway!'

In 1972 Eddie Gilbert was discovered in a mental institution, having spent the past twenty-three years there and being incapable of conversation.

As the nineteenth century entered its final quarter there was not the profusion of fast bowlers that abounded in the previous quarter. Probably the only truly fast bowler between Morley and Tom Richardson was Jack Crossland, of Lancashire, though he was long thought to have an illegal action. Though no umpire no-balled him for throwing, Lord Harris wrote to Lancashire in 1885 stating that Kent would not play Lancashire while they included in their team bowlers whose actions were not above suspicion. He named Crossland and the slow left-arm bowler George Nash. Like

Al Capone, Crossland was eventually trapped on a technicality. It was found that he had broken his residential qualification by living in Nottingham for a few months in 1884, and MCC disqualified him. (Lord Harris himself, incidentally, had an early experience of a cricket ball against his skull when A. G. Bovill, a fast bowler using a wet ball, laid him out in 1871. He remembered nothing until he came to in the dressing-room.)

Among the last of the truly fast roundarm bowlers were the Rev. Robert Lang, who set batsmen atremble in the late 1850s and early 1860s, and Walter Powys, left-arm, who took 24 Oxford wickets in three Varsity matches, 1871-2-4. Lang, whose obituary in *Wisden* rated two whole pages, attracted attention first at Harrow from 1855 to 1859, then at Cambridge, where his bowling and Herbert Marshall's long-stopping to it enchanted onlookers if not the batsmen. It is quite unverifiable, of course, but there were apparently some who felt his pace was greater than that of Jackson and Tarrant. From the age of 22, having represented the Gentlemen, he channelled his energies into his ecclesiastical duties, and was seldom seen in flannels again. Powys, who died at 42, took 6 for 26 and 7 for 49 for Cambridge in the 1872 Varsity match, and received the very considerable tribute from Lord Harris, as late as 1921, that he 'was perhaps as fast as anyone that has ever bowled'. His relatively infrequent participation in top-class cricket denies the opportunity to assess him against others who might have disputed Lord Harris's claim.

One who could have touched the speed of Powys was William Foord-Kelcey, of Oxford and Kent, who once sent a bail 48 yards. A hard-hitting batsman, fine fieldsman, and 'round-armed bowler of great pace', he was a many-sided asset for any team for which he played, and with his giant skipping strides and direction of delivery often around the ribs he was hinted at by one amateur historian as having bowled Bodyline sixty years before the word was coined. Then there was the Rev. F. C. Hope-Grant, who played for Cambridge University in 1863, became chaplain to the

Prince of Wales, and died in 1875 aged only 34. While he played he was feared for his speed. He, like so many others who hammered fingers and shins and split stumps for a brief but thunderous period, is today all but unheard of. Not so F. C. Cobden, who was the central figure in one of the most thrilling finishes of all time. In the 1870 Varsity match at Lord's Oxford, 175 for seven when Cobden began his famous over, needed only four runs to win. A single was taken from the first ball, off the second the batsman was caught, and Cobden bowled the remaining two men with the third and fourth balls to take perhaps the most dramatic hat-trick of all. He was a fast roundarm bowler of whom much must have been expected after this performance, but the rest of his playing career was anticlimax.

On the variable pitches of last century and against the gathering velocity of bowlers it is somewhat surprising that there was not an appallingly long list of serious casualties and fatalities. Perhaps it may be explained by man's instinctive powers of evasion and preparedness to submit to charges of cowardice if absolutely necessary.

As it was, the first-class game served up one solitary martyr to its unspoken peril. In June 1870 a Nottinghamshire side went to Lord's to play MCC. The visitors included Richard Daft (who top-scored in each innings with 117 and 53), Alfred and Jemmy Shaw, William Oscroft, William McIntyre, George Wootton, and a highly promising batsman, a pleasant, slight young man, about to celebrate his 26th birthday, named George Summers, whose score of 41 was second to Daft's. His last scoring stroke was a five from a cut in the direction of the Tavern before he was bowled by a shooter from John Platts, a small but tremendously fast bowler from Derbyshire who could swing the ball pronouncedly.

MCC were fielding a strong side, with Cobden and Tom Hearne assisting the bowling and W. G. Grace, I. D. Walker, C. E. Green, William Yardley, and C. I. Thornton among the batsmen. In reply to Nottinghamshire's 267 they could muster only 183, WG carrying his bat for 117 and Walker making 48. Following on, MCC scored 240, J. W. Dale, stopping incessant shooters, making 90, and Walker 63. WG was bowled by Jemmy Shaw without scoring.

Nottinghamshire, thus set 157 to win, lost their first wicket at 23, and Summers entered, offering the outgoing batsman Oscroft some words of consolation as he passed him : 'Just your luck, Bill, to get out with a hit like that.' (Oscroft once suffered the misfortune of taking a terrible blow in the face while batting at Canterbury, and as he fell to the ground he put his thumb out of joint.)

The first ball to Summers, from Platts, rose steeply, probably having hit a tiny pebble. (Ironically this was the first season in which a heavy roller was used at Lord's, presaging better wickets there and elsewhere that the practice was adopted.) William Yardley, who was keeping wicket for MCC, spoke of that fatal ball in *Talks with Old English Cricketers* : 'If Summers had been able to duck and avoid the ball I must inevitably have got it between the eyes. I have often felt sorry since that it was not I who was struck, for I don't suppose that the result would have been more than a pair of lovely black eyes to me, whereas Summers was struck in a vital part—i.e. on the thinnest part of the temple (other accounts stated the cheekbone), which was fractured by the blow, it appeared, at the post-mortem examination. In all my career I never saw a ball get up with such lightning rapidity. The pitch of the ball and the blow on Summers's head appeared to be simultaneous. . . . The occurrence was the purest accident. When struck Summers reeled like a teetotum, and fell.'

C. I. Thornton, who with Yardley carried Summers down to the parlour of the Tavern, said : 'I always fancy he thought he was settled from the moment the ball struck him. It was a fearful crack on the temple, and when struck he jumped up into the air, and then fell all of a heap. . . . I shall never forget Richard Daft coming in next, with a towel round his head covered with a scarf tied under his chin. The first ball he had pitched about halfway and went clean over his head. He did let Platts have it and no mistake, and the bowler was taken off after that over.'

C. E. Green, from long-stop, had been the first to reach Summers, and WG the first to render medical assistance. He felt his pulse and murmured, 'He is not dead.' Green felt from the way Summers's fists were clenched that he was critically injured. He later also observed, cynically, that Daft, who was 'always dapper and rather full of self-importance' now looked 'ludicrous' in his improvised protective headgear.

George Summers, watched over throughout by Alfred Shaw, was apparently on the road to survival and recovery, and insisted on sitting in the hot sun to see the remainder of the match, which his side won by two wickets (one in reality, since it is inconceivable that Summers would have been allowed to bat).

The tragedy entered its conclusive act when the young man decided to travel back to Nottingham, against the advice of a London doctor. The train journey shook him up badly and, as WG, the cricketing doctor, recalled, 'developed symptoms which subsequently proved fatal' despite the herbal treatment rendered in his hometown. He died of brain concussion on June 19, four days after the match.

MCC purchased a tombstone for his grave in Nottingham General Cemetery 'to mark their sense of his qualities as a cricketer and to testify their regret at the untimely accident at Lord's ground which cut short a career so full of promise'.

As for the wretched bowler, Platts, who thereafter took to slow bowling, WG wrote: 'I shall never forget his mental distraction.'

One hundred and five years later, at Auckland, New Zealand, but for some prompt medical attention, Chatfield and Lever might have re-enacted the horror of that far-off day.

6. AUSSIE THUNDER

Spofforth—Sammy Woods—Albert Trott—'Terror' Turner
'Jonah' Jones

Enter the Australians! Led by Frederick Robert Spofforth
—'Spoff', 'The Demon'—6 ft 3 ins of aggression, with penetrative eyes, eagle-nose, sideburns, Dennis Lillee without
long hair. In 1878, at Lord's during the Australians' first-
ever tour, he stunned the English cricket fraternity by taking
six MCC wickets for four runs in the first innings, including
the hat-trick, and five for 16 in the second to lead a rout of
a distinguished Eleven in one day by nine wickets. It is said
that he was roused to a livid ire by the remark of a member
to his neighbour in the pavilion that he wondered how well
these 'niggers' could play cricket. Spofforth showed him,
as he was to show countless others in his long career.

He began as a raw pace bowler, having been a fast underarm bowler as a boy in Sydney and changing to overarm
after seeing George 'Tear 'em' Tarrant with Parr's 1863–64
team. But soon he perceived the wisdom of extending his
armoury, and he developed a range of deliveries which
included wonderfully deceptive changes of pace, engineered
by varying the amount of ball in his grip. His fastest ball
remained a terror to all batsmen, and his wicketkeepers
would have had an even more unenviable job had he not
devised a system of signalling some of his intentions to them.
Blackham, the great Victorian and Australian wicketkeeper,
with his 6 oz gloves—about a fifth of the weight and size of
modern wicketkeeping gauntlets—was an exhibition in

himself as he darted about to take the Demon's fireballs.

Spofforth did not always believe in Blackham. He withdrew from the first-ever Test match because Billy Murdoch, whom he favoured, was not chosen to keep wicket. But he soon made up for lost time. He played in the second, also at Melbourne in 1877, took 123 wickets in the 19 major matches of his first tour of England the following year—when no Test was played—and in the sole Test match of 1878–79, at Melbourne, he took 13 for 110 in Australia's ten-wicket victory, including the first Test match hat-trick. His victims were Royle, Mackinnon and Tom Emmett. An injured finger kept him from the only Test in England in 1880, and he barely featured in the 1881–82 series—though he apparently bowled down all twenty of his opponents' wickets in an up-country game that season.

By 1882, though, his great moment had arrived. Only one Test was played in England that summer, but it was to become one of the most famous of them all—the 'Ashes Match' at The Oval. One of the few details of that historic contest not to have been repeated *ad nauseam* is that Spofforth, so often compared with Mephistopheles in his appearance and threatening manner, actually attended the fancy dress ball on the voyage to England in Mephistophelean costume. Uncanny.

England needed a mere 85 to win the match, though it had been low-scoring throughout and Spofforth had taken 7 for 46 in the first innings. Yet with 51 on the board with only two men out, an England victory seemed a formality.

There were times during the 1882 tour when it was thought that Spofforth was either a spent force or was not trying—conserving his energy (relating him to some players of today : he physically resembled Lillee, but this fluctuation of mood identifies him with John Snow of Sussex and England). In 1878 he took 763 wickets in Australia, America and England; in 1880 he took 714 in Australia and England, all for an average of around six. Unreasonably, he was judged against these stupendous returns. On the afternoon of August 29, 1882, when the chips were down, he bowled as he had never bowled before.

It sometimes takes an irritant to put that extra yard into a bowler's speed. Spofforth and the rest of the Australians were upset at the manner of young Sammy Jones's dismissal towards the end of Australia's second innings. Jones, having completed a run, left his crease to pat down a bump on the pitch, and W. G. Grace, having taken the return, strode across and removed the bails. Upon appeal, umpire Thoms had no alternative but to give the batsman out 'run out'. Perhaps Jones ought not to have left his crease, particularly with WG in the vicinity; but it was now 'in the book', and the Australians, seeing it as gamesmanship, were fuming.

'This thing can be done!' growled Spofforth, and if it seemed quite unlikely with England 51 for two, the Demon having taken these first two, kept to his word by skittling five more wickets in this innings, snatching a seven-run victory for Australia before an hysterically excited crowd. One man died of a haemorrhage about the time of the end of Australia's innings, and as England trembled to their doom another spectator chewed the head off his umbrella. It was the day in Test match history which deserved television coverage more than any other!

Spofforth, having thought much about the task before him and having slept little overnight, started at a great pace from the gasworks end, and for a time bounced the ball direct at WG's ample figure. Then he cut his pace and began to do things with the ball, his sinister intent advertised by the cluster of close fieldsmen. Wicketkeeper Blackham stood up; Harry Boyle, pioneer of the suicide fielding position, crouched near the striker at silly mid-on; Tom Horan was at backward short leg; the giant George Bonnor was at slip with Sammy Jones; Billy Murdoch and little Alec Bannerman, both of lugubrious countenance, stood square and close in on the off side. There was a cover and a mid-off, and George Giffen was positioned out at long-on to catch any desperate heaves at Spofforth's slower ball.

As WG and Ulyett built England's score, Spofforth switched to the pavilion end in place of Garrett, the fast-medium bowler. The break-through came when Ulyett touched a fast one to Blackham, who held the catch low down. WG went next, caught at mid-off from Harry Boyle's bowling for 32, and a tremor of alarm swept through the English camp. With six wickets remaining, England needed 32 more as the Hon. Alfred Lyttelton went out to join A. P. Lucas, the hour-hand of the clock dropping slowly on to five, the ground becoming firmer for the bowlers. Spofforth and Boyle tightened their grip on the situation. There was an eerie silence about the ground; England's waiting batsmen sat huddled, shivering in the cold air. As maiden over followed maiden only the tinkle of the hansom-cabs outside could be heard.

A stalemate was broken by a tactical ploy. Though England required only 20 to win, the Australians gave a single with a misfield so that the bowlers would have fresh targets. Soon the dividend was delivered. Spofforth charged in on his angled run, eight menacing strides. Over went the arm, and the ball crashed through Lyttelton's guard and took the top of the middle stump. A. G. Steel entered, and had to pass Spofforth's baleful glare as he walked to the crease. Within minutes he was on his way back, caught-and-bowled halfway down the pitch by Spofforth, whose slower ball had claimed another victim. His next ball bowled the local hero Maurice Read. England 70 for seven: 15 needed.

A yorker first ball to Billy Barnes almost did its work, but the batsman chopped down on it. Then three byes drew everyone's attention to the boldness and magnificent teamwork of Spofforth and his wicketkeeper Blackham throughout the innings in having no long-stop despite the delicate position.

The bearded Boyle, medium-pace round the wicket, turning from leg, continued to bowl tightly, and Murdoch stuck to this attack, praying that the burly Barnes would not unleash one or two tension-breaking hoicks through mid-wicket. Then Spofforth broke through again, forcing Lucas to play on to one which turned a lot from outside the off. When Barnes was caught at point off his glove off Boyle,

England were 75 for nine. Edmund Peate, Yorkshire's slow left-arm bowler, came in, his captain, A. N. Hornby, having told him to leave everything to C. T. Studd, one of England's finest batsmen, held back to number ten and now stranded at the non-striker's end. Peate was expected to exercise caution. He had an almighty swing and got two runs. One ball left, then Spofforth would do his worst on Studd. But it never came to that. Peate irresistibly thrashed again ... missed ... and it was all over. England all out 77; Boyle 3 for 19 off 20 four-ball overs, Spofforth 7 for 44 off 28, 14 for 90 in the match. Australia winners by seven runs. Stunned silence at the ground followed by uproar. For the first time, Australia had humbled the full might of England, and small boys were forgiven for believing that F. R. Spofforth had horns in his head.

England regained the newly-created Ashes in Australia that winter, but it was hardly Spofforth's fault. In the Sydney Test, when England's honour was restored, he took 4 for 73 and 7 for 44. The 1884 tour of England brought him over 200 wickets, including an astounding 7 for 3 against an England XI at Birmingham, and at the end of that year he played an important part in Australia's two home wins in the first five-match Test rubber. The 1886 series went resoundingly to England, but Spofforth's sixteen Test wickets were almost as many as the other Australians took between them, though he seemed to have lost something after a hefty drive from Lord Harris injured his right hand.

That summer he married a girl from Derbyshire and took her back to Australia with him, and in the following January, aged 33, he played his final Test match, the thrilling 13-run victory by England at Sydney. And so his career at the highest level was ended: 18 Tests, 94 wickets. There was plenty more cricket in the Demon yet, for Derbyshire and on the London club circuit, but he was mellowing unexpectedly as the years went by. It had always taken a strong man to stand up to him, and the stories of his being at the wrong end of a joke are very few. One concerned umpire Jim Phillips, an Australian who played for Middlesex before joining the ranks of the judiciary. He once no-balled Spofforth for dragging his back foot well over the crease. 'Sorry, Jim. My foot slipped!' explained Spofforth with an evil grin. Next ball, perfectly legitimate, was also called by Phillips, and Spofforth turned upon him and addressed him with a few words chosen at random. 'Sorry, Spoff,' said the umpire blandly, 'my tongue slipped!'

Having qualified for Derbyshire, he played twice against Yorkshire in 1889, taking fifteen wickets in one of these matches, yet his county career was brief: one season as co-captain, and 42 wickets at 11·36—top of the averages, where he always belonged.

He moved to London in 1891 and played some seasons with the star-studded Hampstead side, taking at least fifty wickets per season until he was fifty, once bagging 200 (at 5·90), and even hitting an innings of 155. At Marlow in 1893 he took all ten wickets for 20 (17 for 40 that day), and a year later repeated the feat with 10 for 14. His fierce reputation was an effective part of his repertoire.

He eventually settled in Surrey, living first at Walton-on-Thames and then Long Ditton, where he saw out his days in comfort, showing his chrysanthemums and rising to the position of chairman of the Star Tea Company. He left £164,000, rather more than 'Foghorn' Jackson. Lord Harris visited him in his final illness and the Demon said to him: 'I made my reputation in May; you knocked me out in May (the hand injury); and I shall go out in May.' He died on June 4, 1926, aged 72, and was buried at Brookwood Cemetery.

He was more than an exceptional bowler. He thought deeply about his art and developed it, influencing others. His approach to the crease hardly varied—all arms and legs, and, it was said uncharitably, nose—yet hardly two balls were alike. His slower ball was deadly and his yorker, usually aimed at the off stump 'because they expect it on the leg stump', was horrific. He stooped in delivery but defended this, saying it prevented strain. Perhaps the closest he came to physical damage was when a Yorkshireman rose from the crowd at Sheffield after Spofforth had knocked a few of the local batsmen about and shouted, 'Chain t'long beggar up; he's trying to kill 'em!' It was a miserable task to have to bat against him, and C. B. Fry, the classical Englishman, was reduced to reasoning that 'I formed the useful guiding principle that even a Demon on an evil wicket can only bowl one ball at a time, and if you really look at the ball you have a good chance of playing it.' Logic which was not always enough.

Two Australians whose lives bore similarities to Spofforth's were Sammy Woods, of Cambridge University, Somerset, England, and Australia, and Albert Trott, of Victoria, Middlesex, Australia, and England. Like Spofforth, they finished their days in England, and like him, too, they were masters of change of pace. Both had shocking yorkers which often clean bowled even batsmen who had been emphatically warned by previous victims.

Woods and Trott were both boisterous souls. 'S. M. J.', who captained Somerset, deserves a book to himself, though he put his name to a sketchy yet fun-packed autobiography in 1925, *My Reminiscences*. He played rugby for England, and was branded the Father of Modern Wing Forward Play. He was a pugilist of a kind in his early days in Sydney, and a hero at the Dardanelles in the First World War. He was a practical joker. He enjoyed staying up all night, burying bottles of beer in the ditches of Somerset—to dig them up, to the amazement of companions, while walking out on hot summer days—and he liked hot lobster and champagne for breakfast. One of the most breathtaking sights ever in cricket was Gregor MacGregor's wicketkeeping to Woods for Cambridge, when the Scot stood up for his bowler's fizzing yorkers and kickers. Only once was he hit on the big toe.

Sammy Woods made his mark on English sport, yet he left an elder brother in Australia who might have made an equally forcible impact. He was, Sammy always claimed, an even faster bowler, though less accurate. Once, when an English team was in Sydney, the brother, nicknamed 'Stringy

Bark', came down from the country and amused himself by bowling at the visitors in the nets. His first ball cracked a post in an adjoining net. The next two hit the back-netting on the full. The batsman then retired, saying he had a letter to write to his insurance company. The story goes that when England lost the Test series 'Stringy Bark' said to his brother: 'I told you they would. They don't know the first bloody thing about fast bowling.'

Trott's career was filled with pathos. Rejected by Australia after an amazing beginning in the Test matches of 1894–95, he went to England, joined Middlesex, and became the most successful all-rounder in county cricket at the turn of the century. His action was similar to Spofforth's, though he had not the Demon's great intelligence. Indeed, his batting fell away through a vain, unceasing effort to emulate his historic hit over the Lord's pavilion off M. A. Noble in 1899. Self-control is an essential in all sports, and of that commodity A. E. Trott was under-endowed. When the great days were over, he took to umpiring, but by 1914 dropsy and a fondness for ale had taken their toll on him and his marriage, and he shot himself the day before war broke out.

Of Australia's early fast bowlers, none was truly express until Ernest Jones, who burst upon the scene in the early 1890s. Frank Allan, a tall left-hander, was known as 'the bowler of a century', and must have had a profound impression on his contemporaries even if few today would bring him into any discussion on fast bowlers. He opened the bowling with Spofforth in the famous debacle of MCC in 1878, and took 106 wickets during the tour. Medium-pacers carried the attack, men such as Boyle and Palmer and Giffen, with the sensational duo of Turner and Ferris appearing in the late 1880s, the former fast-medium with uncanny control of length and off-break, the latter left-arm off an idiosyncratic run-up, each bowling into the other's footmarks.

C. T. B. Turner had a springy, graceful approach, and his bowling was once timed at Woolwich Arsenal at 55 mph—not fast, yet still allowing less than a second for the batsman to sight and deal with the ball. When allied to the nagging length and almost infallible 'homing in' on the stumps with turn sometimes wide sometimes not, it may be seen that 'Terror' Turner was at all times an awkward proposition. And there was no escape at the other end, for Ferris was almost as lethal. Figures for once speak loudly and truly: on the 1888 tour of England (when later in the year Jack the Ripper, who was most probably Montague Druitt, a Winchester, Dorset and MCC fast bowler, submitted London to another kind of terror) Turner took 314 wickets at 11·12 and Ferris, merely 21 years old, 220 at 14·10. Two years later they returned to take 215 wickets each. In their eight Tests together they took 104 wickets while the other Australian bowlers managed only 21. Yet Australia lost seven of those contests and won one. It is not always that bowlers win matches. Some runs have to be put on the board, and Australia could not find them in sufficient quantity. England might have known what to expect from these 'terrible twins' after their first Test, at Sydney in 1886–87, when they bowled them out for 45 and 184, taking 17 wickets for 171. Australia still contrived to lose by 13 runs.

Ferris died at 33 while serving in the Boer War. Turner, who reached 101 Test wickets in only 17 Tests before he was rejected during the 1894–95 series, died on New Year's Day, 1944, aged 81. His ashes were to remain in a cardboard box in a funeral parlour in Sydney for 28 years before they were discovered and removed for interment with honour in his hometown of Bathurst.

Another towering figure for a dozen years from 1890 was Hugh Trumble, whose slow to medium off-spinners and variation helped restore Australia's Test match fortunes. His 141 wickets against England remains easily a record for Tests between the two countries. But he does not belong among the fast bowlers. Ernest Jones does. After some years of waiting Australia found her man: tallish, built like a bullock, sometime miner, sometime stevedore, Jones was no intellectual. 'Affie' Jarvis, his wicketkeeper in the South Australian side, soon found the ideal position to stand to his bowling: well, well back. In a club match he once knocked a long-stop off his feet.

They called him 'Jonah', and he had a whale of a time when he reached England in 1896, taking the wickets of W. G. Grace, F. S. Jackson, Shrewsbury, William Gunn, Ranjitsinhji, C. B. Fry, and George Davidson for 84 runs at Sheffield Park, Sussex, and bouncing one of cricket history's most famous balls through WG's beard. When the Champion remonstrated, Jones is said to have retorted, 'Sorry, Doc. She slipped!' WG was lucky: though he did take a few body blows. F. S. Jackson actually had a rib cracked, and was out of cricket for three weeks. When next he met Jones the big Australian apologised and shook his hand. His grip was so crushing that Jackson felt almost as much pain as when hit in the chest.

Jones toured England three times—in 1896, 1899 and 1902 —taking 121, 135 and 71 wickets respectively. He was encouraged to shorten his run early in his career, and became less wild, more thoughtful. Always he was a fearsome proposition on a hard wicket, but on soft wickets he lost much of his penetration. It was his ability to gain sharp lift— rather like Jeff Thomson's—that elevated him above his Australian rivals. A. G. Moyes as a youngster watched him bouncing them at Archie MacLaren at Adelaide, the batsman bowing gracefully beneath the whistling projectile.

C. B. Fry considered Jones the fastest he ever faced over a prolonged period, though England's Kortright took the palm for speed of a single delivery; F. S. Jackson thought Jones the best fast bowler of his time. He was also a magnificent fieldsman at mid-off—practically unpassable.

Batsmen have always moaned and groaned at pitches they considered sub-standard, and so have bowlers, often for different reasons. And when Ernest Jones tried bouncing a ball between overs on the pitch at The Oval, and it barely rose, and he said bitterly 'This is going to ruin cricket' he might have been speaking for bowlers in England in the 1970s; for if a fast bowler can get the ball to lift only bail-high he is discouraged, and is tempted to bowl negatively.

The batsman, too, while feeling in less physical danger, knows that strokes are harder to make. Think, for a moment, where this leaves the spectator!

Jones was, like every great fast bowler, a thrilling sight for any onlooker. There were some, however, who felt that his action was not quite legitimate, and in 1897–98 umpire Jim Phillips was also of this opinion, no-balling him in the State match against Stoddart's XI at Adelaide and again in one of the five Tests. That was all. It may well have been that Jones lapsed in an over-zealous, but probably innocent, extra effort. There was a kind of witch-hunt going on in the 1890s, for several bowlers were obviously in need of check. Such outbreaks of throwing have always called forth courageous umpires, and Phillips was one such.

Among the passions running high during the throwing outburst was that of Spofforth, who went as far as to write (in a letter to *Sporting Life*) that throwing should be legalised: 'in one season it would bring about its own cure.' An alternative, he thought, was to set up a committee, with Lord Harris its chairman, with the power to suspend a player reported for transgressing.

Some bowlers with illegal actions were hounded from the game—fortunately before the greater evil of emulation by the young could take root. Jones survived, and prospered. Even thirty years after his last Test match he was a popular figure at the wharves, one side only of his head having turned grey, welcoming English sides to Australia with stentorian cries of 'You haven't got a chance!' This was the man who, when asked by King Edward VII if he had attended St Peter's College, Adelaide, replied, 'Yes, I drive the dust cart there every week.'

Like so many of the breed, he was good company when he hadn't a cricket ball in his hand and fire in his eyes. He was the first of Australia's great speed bowlers.

7. THREE OF THE BEST

Tom Richardson—Bill Lockwood—S. F. Barnes

Tom Richardson was born in a gypsy caravan, and was born for fast bowling. Huge, mustachio'd, with black ringlets framing his kindly face, he played his first full season with Surrey, in 1893, after startling success with the Mitcham club, taking 174 wickets of which 104 were bowled. He built up his pace off a moderately long run, culminating in a high leap, and his accuracy was a by-word. He bowled a fuller length than most of his kind, getting the ball to veer in from the off through a body action which, like Maurice Tate's in later years, might have offered up an explanation if only analysis had been possible. His greatest weapon, though, was off-cut, or break-back. Every few balls he would rip his fingers across the seam at release point and it would cut in sometimes all of a foot, even on the plumbest wicket. All he needed on top of this armoury was stamina, and in this God-given commodity he was never found lacking.

With around half his matches on the heartless Oval pitches and with only one ball available throughout an innings, he took 290 wickets in 1895, still easily the highest tally for a fast bowler in a season. And some had suspected him of being drained after the strenuous tour of Australia the previous winter!

In 1896 he took 246 wickets, and in 1897, 273. As he had taken 196 in 1894, his haul in four consecutive seasons was a phenomenal 1005 wickets. For this, quite apart from the stories of his wonderful nature, he will stand on a pinnacle as long as people care about cricket.

His two tours of Australia were crowded with tales of his unfailing and heroic endeavour. Under a burning sun, in match after match, bathed in sweat, he carried the attack, never relenting, never allowing the batsmen to relax their vigil, ignoring the protest in his muscles. He was abused at times by crowds who thought he meant ill to their batsmen—and during one Test he had the little Victorian Harry Graham regularly dropping to his knees to avoid decapitation—yet they failed to understand that this lion had the softest, warmest of hearts. Herbert Strudwick, his Surrey wicketkeeper in later seasons, often told of Richardson's reluctance to bowl flat out upon resumption after he had injured a batsman, and A. A. 'Dick' Lilley, who stood up to the stumps when he first kept wicket to him, noted that his pace dropped after a ball had struck him painfully in the chest. WG soon intervened: 'You stand back, Dick, or he won't bowl full out!'

Of all Richardson's gargantuan deeds none was more dramatic than one which ended in futility, in the Test match against Australia at Old Trafford in 1896. Neville Cardus recreated the final moments, after Richardson had striven for 42.3 overs and three hours to bowl England to victory —a victory which might well have been achieved had not wicketkeeper Lilley, towards the end, jarred his elbow after taking a snick from Kelly, Australia's number nine, and spilt the catch. Australia got home by three wickets, and Cardus visualised Richardson, who had taken 13 for 244 off 544 balls in the match: 'His body still shook from the violent motion. He stood there like some fine animal baffled at the uselessness of great strength and effort in this world. ... A companion led him to the pavilion, and there he fell wearily to a seat.'

A less romantic speculation from the pen of another was to the effect that the beloved Tom was first into the pavilion and had sunk two pints before any of the others had taken their boots off! Nevertheless, although he took 5 for 82 and 5 for 37 in the two matches with Middlesex that followed the Test match, it was generally held that he was never quite the force again. And he was only 26.

He must have felt the strain on that great frame of his by the following season, for it was said that he needed extra financial encouragement before agreeing to go with the English team to Australia in the winter of 1897–98.

He was not spared in the wave of 'McCarthyism' that engulfed all bowlers with even a hint of irregularity in their actions, even if, like Ernest Jones, he soon lost his rawness. The murmur may well have started from batsmen simply stunned by his exceptional speed. Fortunately the suspicion did not last.

One area where he soon received a 'clearance' was, of all places, at Bramall Lane, Sheffield, where the locals were tough, discriminating, and Yorkshire-minded. Richardson had been pummelling their batsmen's hands, arms, thighs, ribs and chests, to cries of 'Take him off!' 'Where's a doctor?' and 'Fetch the ambulance!' Finishing with 9 for 47 in the first innings, he batted in his customary position of number ten, and heard the grinders call out to Hirst to give him a taste of his own medicine. Hirst's third ball whipped in and smacked Richardson on the thigh to a deafening roar from the outer. All the same, when the Rev. R. S. Holmes enquired of the noisy spectators whether they thought the Surrey bowler's action was legitimate or a throw his answer was a chorus: 'We wish the booger did throw; he wouldn't be the booger he is!'

If a man is to be judged on figures, and if those figures are to reflect his performance at the highest level, then Richardson's Test figures against Australia are worth examining. In fourteen consecutive matches between 1893 and 1897–98 his striking rate was astonishing: at Old Trafford—ten; in five Tests in Australia—six, seven, eight, two, nine; in England in 1896—eleven, thirteen, none (this the Oval Test, when he and four other professionals went on strike for £20 instead of the regular £10—Abel, Hayward and Richardson relenting and playing after all); and in the gruelling

1897–98 tour of Australia—five, one, four, two, and, ending as he began, ten, including 8 for 94 in the first innings. In fourteen Tests, when Australia's batting consisted of Gregory, Darling, Hill, Bannerman, Lyons, Giffen, the Trotts, Bruce, Graham, Iredale and Noble, he took 88 wickets. The last few were taken in spite of painful rheumatism and increasing weight and in searing heat.

He saw out his playing days with Somerset, and spent his precious few years of retirement as a publican. When he died in 1912 while on holiday in France he was still only 41. It is thought his heart failed him—something that he had never allowed while there were more wickets to be taken, even though he may have bowled twenty, twenty-five, thirty-five overs already. The Gentlemen v Players match at The Oval was suspended on the Saturday afternoon of his funeral at Richmond, and grief was felt by all who had ever known him or watched him play cricket.

He was a formidable bowler, yet how hopeless it must have seemed for most of the batsmen opposed to Surrey or England during the 1890s when at the other end William Henry Lockwood was bowling. Here was the first great fast bowling combination, the earliest example of pace bowlers of rare hostility and endurance *hunting as a pair*, rendering batting a pretentious if not futile pastime.

Lockwood was Nottingham-born, but after a handful of matches for his native county he moved, at the age of nineteen, to Surrey and qualified. Five years later, in 1892, having studied the wonderful pace-changes of George Lohmann and developed his speed to well above average, he emerged as the most successful bowler in England, with 114 wickets in sixteen Championship matches. Like Richardson, he brought the ball back abnormally from the off, and like no-one else in the world he could hold a ball back in the air without any noticeable change in action. He was also a master at using the full width of the crease, which was not as wide in those days.

Here was a stupendous pair of fast bowlers.

C. B. Fry, whose erudition in these and most other

matters was seldom questioned, rated Lockwood ahead even of Richardson. And the handsome Nottingham man could bat well, too!

But one thing separated them, to Lockwood's discredit. He was temperamental to the point where on a number of occasions he gave of less than his best. This is not an unfamiliar tale across the years. He also suffered more than average from strains and injuries; indeed, at times he seemed accident-prone, having a hand slashed by a bursting soda siphon, ricking a shoulder, and almost drowning while on a harbour cruise—all during the 1894–95 tour of Australia— a tour which he and his followers wished to forget in almost every detail. Lockwood was now in eclipse. Yet his career was in two parts, and when Richardson had finally burned himself out after his second tour, in 1897–98, Lockwood came again, his failures and his personal tragedies (the death of his wife and child and naturally taken his mind off everything else) placed behind him.

For around five years from 1898 Bill Lockwood was England's finest bowler, sometimes carrying a thigh injury but invariably troubling batsmen even of the highest class. In the final Test of 1899 he took seven Australian wickets for 71 and looked a class above his fellows, who happened to be the fiery W. M. Bradley, A. O. Jones, F. S. Jackson, leg-spinner Townsend, and young Wilfred Rhodes. This was probably Lockwood's greatest performance, but it was interrupted by the offending thigh muscle, and he had to leave the field during Australia's follow-on.

He might well have gone to Australia again in 1901–02, but there was doubt about his physical survival, and Archie MacLaren took S. F. Barnes, who appeared almost from nowhere, having played only three times for Warwickshire and three times for Lancashire in the preceding seven seasons. Barnes went on to establish a reputation as perhaps the greatest bowler of all time, bowling very fast when it suited him but more often spinning the ball all ways at a brisk medium pace. A difficult man to handle, he growled, scowled and smiled his way through 27 Tests—it could have been so many more—taking 189 wickets at 16·43, marginally under C. T. B. Turner's average and second to none, other than George Lohmann's 112 at 10·75, among major Test match bowlers. Even in the year of his death, in 1967, at the age of 94, Barnes spoke of his conviction that had he been playing in modern times, with perhaps an average of eight Test matches a year, he would have taken around 500 Test wickets! Much, one feels, would have depended upon his relationship with his captain and chairman of selectors.

Lockwood, at the age of 34, came back to play in four of the Tests against Australia in the eventful 1902 series and finished top of England's bowling with 17 wickets at 12·11. Since he did not get on in the first Test, when Australia were dismissed by Hirst and Rhodes for 36 at Edgbaston, and the second Test was washed out with England 102 for two, all seventeen of his wickets were taken in the fourth and fifth matches. (He was omitted from the third.) He took 6 for 48 (after being unable to bowl on the slippery turf before lunch) and 5 for 28 at Old Trafford, where Australia stole a famous victory by three runs, and one for 85 and 5 for 45 in the familiar surroundings of The Oval, where England got home by one wicket in the thriller which became known as 'Jessop's match' after the Croucher's 75-minute century on the last day. That was the end of Lockwood's Test career. In 1904 he and Richardson played their last together for Surrey.

They came to a powerful Surrey eleven and extended its term of success. The county were champions in 1887, 1888, 1889 (equal), 1890, 1891 and 1892, fifth in 1893, first again in 1894 and 1895, fourth in 1896, runners-up in 1897, fourth in 1898, and champions for the ninth time in thirteen seasons in 1899. Others, chiefly Yorkshire, took over from there, but that glorious period in Surrey's cricket history is emblazoned with the names of the Reads, Abel (who made thousands of runs against fast bowling despite alleged poor eyesight and a tinge of cowardice), Hayward, Brockwell,

81

Lohmann, Key, and Harry Wood, the reliable wicketkeeper. Most of the drama, however, was supplied by Richardson and Lockwood, as fine looking a pair as ever bowled together.

Comparison between them is not easy. In *Ten Great Bowlers* Ralph Barker assembled the recorded views of a number of the major batsmen of the day, and opinion was just about divided. Ranjitsinhji, Murdoch and Fry insisted that Lockwood was the more dangerous. Ranji wrote: 'It was possible to be 120 not out on a plumb wicket and then to be clean bowled by Lockwood and walk away to the pavilion not knowing what one would have done if one had another chance at the ball.'

George Lohmann rated Richardson the best in the world *on a good wicket*, pointing out that he had difficulty with his footholds on wet pitches. G. L. Jessop expressed the greatest admiration for Richardson too, and C. J. Kortright —one of the candidates for the title 'fastest of all time', of whom more anon—as an old man recalled Richardson as 'the finest bowler I ever saw'. Wicketkeeper Lilley named him as the greatest fast bowler to whom he had ever kept wicket. George Giffen, Australia's great all-rounder, likened Richardson to Spofforth.

Lockwood, unlike the partner with whom he will always be associated, was also a very good batsman, probably the best ever among England fast bowlers. In 1902, his wonderful year, he took 2 for 43 and 7 for 63 for the Players against a dazzlingly strong Gentlemen side at Lord's and hit 100 in between. The Players won by an innings, and had not Len Braund also scored a century and taken seven wickets the match would have gone down positively as 'Lockwood's match'. He made the extraordinarily high number of fifteen centuries in first-class cricket.

Richardson died relatively young; Lockwood, having moved back to Radford, Nottingham, was crippled by arthritis for the final few years of his life, but was often seen at Trent Bridge, sitting in his wheelchair near the sightscreen. It was from this vantage point that he passed judgment on the new fast bowling sensation of the late 1920s, Harold Larwood, whom he considered as fast as anyone in his own day—except for his old comrade, the kindly dark-eyed Tom Richardson.

8. THE FASTEST?

In 1883 a ball bowled by Merritt Preston killed Albert Luty in a local 'Derby' in the Yorkshire village of Yeadon. York-shire cricket enthusiast Ron Yeomans, visiting the local churchyard eighty years later, found the graves of bowler and slain batsman within a pitch-length of each other, the sexton explaining that after the accident Preston was never the same man. He pointed to another grave and said: 'There's the man who caught Luty as he dropped, Charlie Dawson. He was the Yorkshire stumper and played against the Australians years ago, when Yeadon beat them.' Albert Luty had been married only a week before.

There are several other cricketers buried at Yeadon, the most famous being Edmund Peate, the slow left-arm bowler whose wicket gave Australia the Ashes in the historic 1882 Test. (Peate began as a fast bowler, and actually made his name with a troupe of touring Clown Cricketers.) Down in Essex, at Fryerning, are buried—also only twenty or so yards apart—A. P. Lucas, one of the most stylish batsmen of the late nineteenth century, and Charles Jesse Kortright, who was a veritable thunderbolt of a bowler during the 1890s. So many eminent cricketers of his time have stated their belief that no-one could ever have been faster that it would be a monotony to list them. Yet for one reason or another he never played for England.

'Korty' was a dedicated cricketer all his life, from the days at Brentwood School (he later went to Tonbridge) when he crept out through his window at four in the morning to play cricket against the chapel wall until reveille at seven. Whenever he could not hold a cricket ball he would take up largish stones and hurl them at trees or lamp-posts, building up the muscles in his hand, arm and shoulder and developing his senses of distance and timing. With his acute sense of competitiveness he was destined to be an athlete out of the ordinary. He confessed in an article in *Wisden* (1948) that he was always wanting to project things farther and faster than anyone else. At the same time he condemned latter-day bowlers for their general unwillingness to practise and for the blame they attached to 'shirt-front' wickets. 'There were many such pitches in my playing days,' he wrote, 'the sort on which if we could bounce the ball bail-high we thought ourselves pretty clever. Yet every county fielded two, sometimes three, genuinely fast bowlers, who were not discouraged by the wickets.'

He once found a pitch, at Wallingford in a club match, which had bounce in it, and so muscularly did he plunge one delivery into it that the ball rose sheer over batsman and wicketkeeper and crossed the boundary on the full— probably the only known instance of a six in byes.

He believed in bowling as fast as possible, straight at the off stump, and without wasting too many balls in short-pitched deliveries (he often advised Essex and England fast bowler of the 1930s, Ken Farnes, to save his energy and pitch the ball further up). He scoffed at the moderns who theorised about and believed in swing and cut. To him fast bowling was a simple exercise.

He once bowled William Gunn in a Gentlemen v Players match at Lord's with a ball which that tall and hungry batsman described as the fastest by a yard of any he had ever received, and W. G. Grace, whose magnificent bat rendered his stumps and his person almost untouchable, was at least once badly mauled by the Essex express. Feelings ran high during one Gloucestershire–Essex match, and the two great amateurs ended not speaking to each other. Happily the feud was patched up only a few days later, and in a most dramatic scenario. It was the Gentlemen v Players match at Lord's, beginning on WG's fiftieth birthday, July 18, 1898. The Gentlemen eventually needed 296 to win, but were reduced to 77 for seven when the bruised but defiant Grace entered. Two more wickets soon fell, and Kortright came out, last man, with seventy-odd minutes remaining. They held out amid mounting tension, the Doctor resolute as ever, his number eleven surprising everyone with his restraint. Eventually Lockwood came up for the final five-ball over. The third was held back a shade, Kortright lofted it over cover, and Schofield Haigh ran for it and caught it, winning the match for the professionals with around two minutes to spare. WG's arm was linked through Kortright's as they left the field in a moment of glory.

Kortright stood six feet tall and, like Lockwood at his peak, had a superb physique, and, like Richardson, enormous reserves of stamina. His run was long—*Cricket* said 'exceptionally long' at fifteen yards!—and wicketkeepers stood a fair distance back from him if they were to take the ball with any degree of comfort. Yet Harry Martyn, the brilliant Somerset 'keeper, is said to have taken up position at the stumps when first he kept to Kortright, in a Gentlemen v Players match. The bowler did not like this and uttered words of warning; Martyn stood his ground, gathered the first of Kortright's rockets right-handed outside the off stump, and tossed the ball back to the bowler so swiftly that it hit the poor unprepared fellow in the chest.

Surrey suffered before his ferocity as much as any county. At Leyton in 1893 he took 8 for 29 and 5 for 35, bowling unchanged through both innings with Walter Mead, and at the same ground two seasons later he took six wickets for four runs. In 1900 he shook the powerful Yorkshire side with 8 for 57. Looking back on those days, he spoke out for his contemporaries, reminding their descendants that in those olden times the fast bowlers had a larger ball to use —not so easy to get the fingers around—a smaller crease— reducing the variations possible in the angle of delivery— and smaller stumps—the drawback here being all too obvious. All of this might have persuaded a man of Kortright's pragmatic outlook to take up batting, and indeed he started with Essex more as a likely 'willow-wielder', scoring 158 in an hour and three quarters at Southampton in 1891, and nine years later slamming 131 out of 166 against Middlesex at Leyton—this despite his advice to bowlers, received earlier from the illustrious Alfred Shaw himself, that it is better not to bat too long when one soon has to bowl. 'We lose that freshness in ourselves, and that suppleness in the fingers which helps so much in bowling.'

Kortright seems not to have stayed too long at the batting crease, even when making a hundred!

The yorker, possibly named after a master at Rugby School, has always been one of the fast bowler's chief weapons, and Kortright used it better than most. His first 'bowled' victim in county cricket, Billy Brockwell, was defeated by a snorter into the base of the stumps. Kortright claimed that the force of impact sent the bails flying forward, 'one breaking as it flew over my head'. On another occasion he remembered a yorker rebounding from the stumps and travelling back past the bowler's wicket almost to the boundary.

One of the most unusual jousts of the 1890s must have been Kortright v Abel. The little Surrey run-accumulator moved towards square leg to play fast bowling, often with a horizontal bat. P. A. Perrin, Essex's prolific batsman, used to recall how Kortright lost his temper: 'It was bad enough when Abel ran away and chopped yorkers off the middle stump through the slips; but when he ran away so far that he *cut* him inside the leg stump and to the left of the wicket-keeper for four "Korty" really did say something.'

It is a great sadness that there are no photographs of Kortright in the classic *Great Bowlers and Fielders: Their*

Methods at a Glance by George W. Beldam and Charles B. Fry, published in 1907. Among its 464 action pictures are several of an elderly Spofforth, two of Tom Richardson (one conveying the force of his final leap and minimising the middle-age spread so very evident in the other photo), and an unworthy picture of Lockwood.

Of the rest in the section devoted to fast bowlers, the most remarkable is of Sammy Woods, with his head *horizontal* just as the ball has left his hand, and the most exciting are of Walter Brearley, George Hirst, 'Tibby' Cotter, and J. J. Kotze. (For the record, the others depicted in this category are Arnold Warren of Derbyshire, who took the wickets of Trumper (twice), Noble, Armstrong, Darling and Laver in his one Test match, in 1905; Walter Lees of Surrey, 'faster than he looks'; Tom Wass of Notts, a spidery bowler of genuine leg-breaks at a distinctly fast pace; Arthur Fielder of Kent, who moved the ball away 'with the arm' and took all ten Gentlemen's wickets for the Players at Lord's in 1906; the lanky H. Hesketh Prichard of Hampshire; G. A. Wilson of Worcestershire; Bill Bestwick, Derbyshire's 'double-jointed' fast bowler; George Thompson, who 'made' Northamptonshire cricket; George Gill of Somerset and Leicestershire; J. H. Hunt of Middlesex; Ernest Smith of Yorkshire, with his 'strong, whizzing flight'; and Alex Kermode, Lancashire's Australian. The actions of all are analysed vividly. There was no shortage of fast and fast-medium bowlers at the dawn of the new century.)

Brearley, like Kortright (who proudly claimed never to have done a day's work in his life), was an amateur, and he left behind a fund of outrageous quotes that possibly drown his statistical achievements in a foam of humour. Beldam and Fry referred to him as 'the fastest bowler at present playing county cricket', and noted that his speed came from sheer strength. He had much stamina, and therefore joins the Class 1 bowlers. He took a deliberate striding run of moderate length, beginning with a curious sideway step to the left, something in the manner of Pakistan's glamorous opening bowler of the 1970s, Asif Masood. Ignoring pace-change, swerve and swing, he relied mainly on varying his angle of attack, using the full width of the crease.

Neville Cardus knew him well, and it is our good fortune and was surely to Brearley's gratification that he did, for most of the Tales of Brearley, apocryphal and otherwise, were inscribed by his fellow Lancastrian. Cardus once scripted him thus: 'Ah hit George Hirst bang on kneecap; and Ah'll swear to mi dying day he was in front—ball would a'knocked all three wickets down. But umpire gives it "not out", and then George hits mi over ropes and crowd, sarcastic-like, shouts, "Ow's that, Maister Brearley?" and next ball he hits me again over ropes, and crowd shouts, "Ow's that?" again, so Ah knocks his middle stump flying in two, and Ah runs down pitch and picks up broken halves of wicket and Ah brandishes 'em at crowd. And then Ah runs off field and comes back with six new stumps and gives 'em to umpire and says, "Here, take these, you'll need all bloody lot before Ah've done." And he needed four on 'em, Ah can tell you.'

In that precious little book *Days in the Sun*, Cardus wrote: 'Every ball was a crisis as far as Brearley was concerned.... There was no end to his energy.... Brearley wallowed in work, indulged it out of pride of his giant's strength, out of the joy that the lusty play of thew and sinew brings, out of desire for masterfulness.' Turning to his batting: 'Brearley could not bat, but how he enjoyed his walk to the wicket!'

Many of his opponents must have enjoyed, or at least felt relief, at their walk *from* the wicket after Brearley at his best had dealt with them, as in 1908, his best season, when he took 163 wickets. Three years earlier he had distinguished himself repeatedly—in dismissing Australia's genius Victor Trumper six times, in taking 7 for 104 for the Gentlemen against the Players on a slow Lord's pitch, and in his demoralisation of Somerset at Old Trafford, where he took 9 for 47 and 8 for 90 in the match, bowling the last two batsmen in the first innings with consecutive balls and taking the first two wickets in the second innings also consecutively, giving him four in four.

He played only four times for England : against Australia twice in 1905 and once in 1909, and in one Test against South Africa in the 1912 Triangular Tournament, taking seventeen wickets in all. Often in his retirement he must have wondered how he came to represent his country on so few occasions. Indeed, Cardus often saw him gazing, in later years, through the Long Room windows at Lord's, at some fast bowler or other. 'He could seldom bear to look for long,' wrote the most imaginative of all cricket-writers; 'his eyes popped almost out of his head; the explosive red of his face heightened. "Ah could throw mi hat down the pitch quicker!" he would say.'

Brearley succeeded in the Lancashire eleven one of the most controversial fast bowlers of them all, Arthur Mold, Northamptonshire-born and a man of uncompromising, even predatory, looks whatever his inner warmth may have amounted to. Throughout his career he was spoken of in some quarters as a thrower, and his critics had their justification in 1900 when Jim Phillips no-balled him at Trent Bridge. A year later, by which time the county captains at their meeting had condemned his action by eleven votes to one, Mold was called by Phillips sixteen times in ten overs in the Lancashire v Somerset match at Old Trafford. Phillips showed great courage in proclaiming his doubts at Mold's home ground, as he had in the case of Ernest Jones at Adelaide, C. B. Fry at Hove, and E. J. Tyler, a slow left-arm bowler, at Taunton. With these calls of 'no-ball', Phillips was writing finis to Mold's career. The bowler was quoted later as having said that he wished he had given up the game before his first-class career had developed, since his being 'called' as a thrower discredited all his great performances.

And there were some astonishing returns by Arthur Mold between 1889 and 1900. Seventeen times he took eight or nine wickets in an innings for Lancashire and for the Lyric Club he took 9 for 43 against the 1890 Australians; fourteen times he took thirteen, fourteen or fifteen wickets in a match for his county. In six matches he bowled unchanged throughout with Johnny Briggs, the little left-arm spinner, and once he bowled remorselessly through both innings of Yorkshire at Huddersfield with Alec Watson. Against Nottinghamshire in 1895 he took four wickets in four balls, and at The Oval in the following season he sent one of George Lohmann's bails almost three pitch-lengths (63 yards 6 inches). In minor cricket he was either formidable or devastating.

All this came from an approach of only four long strides, but his body swing was impressive and, according to 'Plum' Warner, who also happened to believe that Mold threw, 'beautiful'. His off-break, or breakback, came off at lightning speed, and Wilfred Rhodes, even when in his nineties, patted his thigh tenderly at the thought of Mold's pace and said that when you were hit by him it was 'like a knife turning in your flesh'.

W. G. Grace thought Mold was 'the fairest of bowlers', and C. B. Fry in his illustrative volume *The Book of Cricket* paid him unequivocal credit, but S. H. Pardon, editor of *Wisden*, saw him only as an illegal interloper on the cricket field. Judgment can hardly be passed at this late stage.

There is only one judgment possible upon George Herbert Hirst of Yorkshire and England: he was the complete all-rounder, a pioneer of marked swerve, and a model professional—loyal, a fighter, a staunch companion and worthy opponent.

He was born at Kirkheaton, as was his slow-bowling partner Wilfred Rhodes, and for years the amusing answer to the question 'Who is the world's best all-rounder?' was to the effect that he batted right-hand, bowled left-, and came from Kirkheaton.

Hirst's output over forty years from 1889 for Yorkshire was prodigious. He made 32,231 runs at the considerable average of 33·96, with 56 centuries (the highest 341 against Leicestershire in 1905, still a Yorkshire record); he took 2569 wickets at 17·86; and he was an unpassable mid-off, taking 550 catches, mainly in that position from stinging drives. In 1906 he astonished all and sundry by doing a 'double double'—2385 runs and 208 wickets in a season—something never done by anyone else and never to be beaten until such time as the English county programme may be reshaped. When anyone asked Hirst if he thought his achievement might be emulated he was accustomed to replying, 'I don't know, but if anyone does he will be very tired.' Much the same answer was given by Fred Trueman, only with some strong adjectival dressing, when asked if anyone was likely to overtake his Test record of 307 wickets.

To consider Hirst for his bowling: he often created panic by sending the ball on a line around a foot outside the off stump only for it to swerve sharply and late right across the batsman, holding a leg-side course to the wicketkeeper's left. It was a delivery once described as seeming like a fast throw-in from cover-point, and if it started wide enough or veered rather less than usual it was apt to smack the batsman's thigh or beat a loud clanging tattoo on his protective box, spreading mirth to all but the victim.

When he gave it full throttle he could bowl at a very lively pace, and even on damp or muddy wickets he could maintain a steady footing, a facility which must have owed much to his squat shape. He was an immensely powerful figure, yet his broad body was surmounted by kindly features and a smile which his county captain Lord Hawke described as going right round his head and meeting at the back. Certainly he was considerate and a man of principle, and was never seen to act in an uncharitable manner other than to get batsmen out or to stop them making runs.

Despite his repeated successes, which gradually made him a legend, Hirst was not an outstanding success in Test cricket, either in England or Australia, where he toured twice. In 1902 he made his biggest marks on international cricket, taking 3 for 15 while Rhodes took 7 for 17 in bowling Australia out for 36 in the Edgbaston Test, then taking 5 for 9 (F. S. Jackson 5 for 12) in Yorkshire's dismissal of the Australians for 23. In the famous Oval Test which concluded the series he made a priceless 58 not out after Jessop had made his immortal 75-minute century, winning the match for England by one wicket by finding the remaining fifteen runs when last man Rhodes joined him. Hirst's innings is in the shadow of Jessop's, and further back in those shadows are his other accomplishments in the match —a first innings of 43 (top score) and six wickets, all prized (Trumper, Duff, Hill twice, Darling and Gregory).

Probably the most outstanding example of his all-round abilities was in Yorkshire's match against Somerset at Bath in 1906, the year of his 'double double': he scored 111 and 117 not out and took 6 for 70 and 5 for 45. His second century came in 66 minutes. Two years later he and Haigh upended Northamptonshire for 27 and 15, Hirst 12 for 19. None of this changed his cap size.

He coached at Eton for eighteen years and was most popular there, and was one of the professional cricketers MCC honoured with honorary life membership in 1949. A box-denter he may have been, but no more pleasant man ever trod a cricket field.

His hunting partner in so many matches was Schofield Haigh, who had a slinging action and took a huge proportion of his wickets with yorkers. Indeed, his percentage of 'bowled' victims is probably higher than that of anyone else. His pace was hardly above medium, which could also be said of the Australian master bowler and tactician M. A. Noble, who learned much about aerodynamics from his days as a baseball pitcher. After Jones, the next express bowler to emerge from the Australian ranks was Albert 'Tibby' Cotter, whose action must have resembled Jeff Thomson's in the present-day Australian XI in that he threw his bowling arm backwards towards mid-off before swishing it through in delivery. This slinging action, combined with a drop of the left shoulder, propelled the ball at a lowish trajectory which had the effect of hurrying it through, much as Larwood and Griffith were able to do in later generations. Cotter began with a very long run-up, but later cut this down with profit, again to link him with another of later times, just as Tyson did in 1954–55. The shorter run somehow increased Cotter's ability to cut the ball back from off.

He was a magnificent specimen of manhood, remembered many years later by Bert Oldfield, who had been a youngster in the Sydney suburb of Glebe when Cotter was at his peak, as muscular and lithe, 'with bright eyes and a smooth creamy skin'. He had a habit of breaking stumps and knuckles, and A. G. Moyes recalled in *Australian Bowlers* how fearsome Cotter could be with a wind behind him. Against South Australia 'the ball flew fast and high, too fast indeed for one batsman, who could only turn his back and take the full force of the ball, which burrowed into his flesh and left a hole into which the ball could have been placed some time later.'

Moyes remembered his ability to get lift occasionally, even from a ball fairly well up. He remembered too his willingness to bowl for hour after hour, 'wringing the perspiration out of his cap', and his certainty of foothold even on wet surfaces, and calling 'Good shot!' if he was hit for four—'an expression of appreciation, and not the signal to expect one at your head next ball.'

He toured England in 1905 and 1909, but was one of the six dissidents who withdrew from the 1912 tour over a dispute with the Australian Board of Control. Yet in his two tours he left a strong impression, particularly in 1905, when he took 124 wickets at under twenty apiece. He played in only the first Test and the last two of the series, and took only four wickets in the first and none in the fourth. Yet his hostility in the opening contest, at Trent Bridge, caused England batsmen and English spectators much discomfort. He thundered in and rocketed the ball down to a wicket-keeper who had to take many balls high above his head. His speed and skill were put into figures eventually in the last Test, at The Oval, where he took 7 for 148 in England's first innings of 430, and two wickets in the second, on a pitch offering him no assistance. 'Some of us got some rib-ticklers,' wrote C. B. Fry, who made 144 in the first innings.

He recorded two outstanding returns during the Tests of 1909—5 for 38 at Leeds, where he wrapped up England's innings 127 runs short of the 214 needed for victory, bowling Fry, Hobbs, Sharp, and Hirst and having Lilley lbw, and 6 for 95 at The Oval, his victims including an illustrious fivesome in Spooner, MacLaren, Rhodes, Woolley (on debut), and Hutchings. This was the match in which England curiously chose only Jack Sharp of Lancashire to support S. F. Barnes above medium-pace, and Sharp made a century.

At home in Australia he was reliable, in the Tom Richardson manner, turning in occasional shock spells, but failed to dominate visiting sides as one of the truly greats would have done. In the 1910–11 series against South Africa he took 22 wickets, but at the high cost of 28·77. This was the season of Aubrey Faulkner, who made 732 runs in the five Tests. It was also the season of Bill Whitty, of South Australia, who took 37 wickets in the series with left-arm fast bowling which, in Sheffield Shield matches, even Victor Trumper found unplayable at times. In ten encounters Whitty dismissed him seven times and in the other three he was not out.

Whitty, an Australian counterpart to George Hirst with his swing and variations, had a pleasing action and a ready tongue. Once refused an appeal for caught behind, he soon bowled a widish ball well clear of the batsman and appealed again. The umpire rebuked him, but he came back with an acid 'Just thought you might make two mistakes in one day!'

In the second Test of the 1910–11 series against South Africa, at Melbourne, Whitty took 6 for 17 off sixteen overs, demolishing the visitors for 80 when, in a high-scoring match, they needed but 170 to win. He toured England in 1909 and 1912, taking most wickets for Australia (25) on the latter tour, and lived till 1974, the last of Australia's pre-First World War Test cricketers.

'Tibby' Cotter, in contrast, did not survive the War. During the advance on Beersheba in 1917 the Australian Light Horse were held in the trenches; Cotter wanted to verify

95

what he saw through his periscope, raised his handsome head, and was shot through the forehead.

The first of South Africa's notable fast bowlers was James J. 'Kodgee' Kotze, who was another who had barely any chance to burn his name across the annals of Test cricket: he played only three times for his country, in 1902–03 against Australia, and in one match against England on the 1907 tour, the last of his three tours of the Old Country. Yet he often bowled at a blistering pace, and was rated by 'Plum' Warner and others as second only to Kortright in speed in the history of the game to date.

A burly man, Kotze took a long and energetic run to the wicket and leapt in a frightening (to some batsmen) manner as he cocked his right arm. He appeared to hold the ball—which he gripped uniquely between thumb and forefinger—just a little longer than most bowlers before release, and this was thought to give it greater thrust. Certainly he achieved an immensely powerful dispatch of the ball, and it hit the pitch with a whack. It swung too, a natural effect stemming from his body swing. He was accurate enough to have Halliwell, the South African wicketkeeper, standing over the stumps and even making leg-side stumpings for him, another example of a 'keeper's skill being brought out by express bowling. Halliwell is thought to have put raw beefsteak into the palms of his wicketkeeping gloves.

In *The Book of Cricket* P. F. Warner stated that Kortright's muzzle velocity was about 2000 feet per second, which equals around 1363 mph, while the speed of Jones, Kotze and Cotter was about 1950 feet per second. This must have been a twelvefold exaggeration at least, but one assumes that cricket's greatest-ever devotee was drawing a quaint kind of comparison. All four may well have approached 100 mph at their peaks, with a tailwind. But we shall never know.

What is known is that Kotze could be as fast at the end of the day as at the beginning, but Samson's strength was not always matched by the heart of an African lion, for Kotze often became despondent if slip catches went down.

Top: John Willes (1777-1852), all-round sportsman, possibly astride the horse which carried him from Lord's in 1822 in high dudgeon after he was no-balled for bowling roundarm. *Bottom left:* Rev. Walter Marcon (1824-1875), of furious speed. He broke a batsman's leg and knocked the bat of another through the wicket. *(MCC Collection) Bottom right:* Alfred Mynn (1807-1861), 'the Lion of Kent'. 'The very earth seemed to tremble under his measured, manly, and weighty stride'.

Top left: John 'Foghorn' Jackson (1833-1901), Nottinghamshire's demon bowler. *Top right:* George Freeman (1844-1895), considered by W. G. Grace to be the best bowler he faced. *(Ron Yeomans) Bottom:* George 'Tear 'em' Tarrant (1838-1870), 'all over the place like a flash of lightning'.

Top left: Woods and Cumbernatch. West Indian forerunners of Hall and Griffith. *Right:* Learie Constantine (1902-1971) – verve and volatility. *Bottom left:* Eddie Gilbert (b1912) – extraordinary Aborigine.

Top: Ken Farnes (1911-1941) bowls Woodfull, 'the unbowl-able', during his ten-wicket Test debut at Trent Bridge in 1934. *(Central Press)* *Bottom:* Bill Bowes (b1908) repeats the miracle, bowling Woodfull for nought at Leeds in the fourth Test of the series. *(Sport & General)*

The flowing perfection of Ray Lindwall (b1921), pride of Australia. Batsmen sweated and quaked; boys tried to emulate. *(Pix, Australia)*

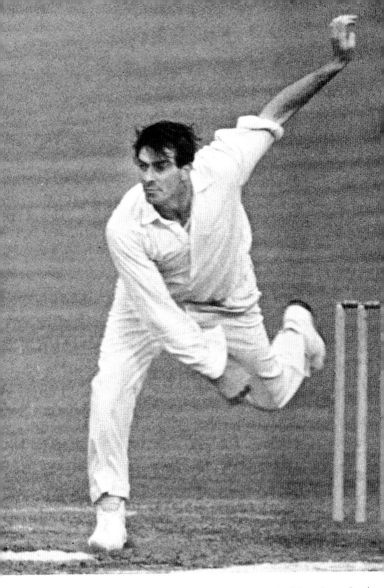

Fred Trueman (b 1931). The ball has been launched, but the action is not done yet. The follow-through will last awhile and the bowler's own summary will be worth hearing! *(Patrick Eagar)*

Top: The exceptional strength and thrust of Frank Tyson (b1930), who surely bowled as fast as any man in history. *(Daily Mirror)* *Bottom:* Alan Davidson (b1929), fast left-arm over the wicket. Will it dip in or run to slip? *(Press Association)*

Top: Ken Barrington clamps his teeth against the agony that always threatens. Adcock bowled this ball, which hammered the England batsman's ribs. *Bottom:* Impassive Brian Close faces a bumper barrage from Mike Holding during the third Test against West Indies at Old Trafford 1976. Sheer bravery! *(Patrick Eagar)*

One of his colleagues, Maitland Hathorn, summed it up nicely, though, by suggesting that 'had he been able to stand in the slips against his own bowling I feel sure he would have been more charitable to the unfortunate fieldsman'.

Fast bowlers make the stomach tingle when they run amok among batsmen; they give wicketkeepers and slip fieldsmen the chance to catch the eye as well as the ball; and, perhaps most exciting of all, they occasionally provide the opportunity for magic innings such as could never be made from the weak clay of medium-pace bowling. Such a situation arose when Ranjitsinhji batted against Kotze in full flow, glancing him, hooking him, evading him. Then in 1904, during the final match of the tour, Jessop hit Kotze's bowling to all parts in making 159 not out for the South of England at Hastings, forcing him to have four men in the longfield.

He toured England in 1901, 1904 and 1907, and enjoyed much success until the last tour, when South Africa relied principally on the googly quartet of Schwarz, Vogler, White and Faulkner.

Kotze was a poor batsman and a handicap in the field, and the most outstanding recollection of him with the bat was that his was the decisive wicket in the South Africans' thrilling tie with Middlesex in 1904, Albert Trott sending his middle stump flying in a cloud of dust.

He died 'with dramatic suddenness' at Cape Town, where he had been groundsman at Newlands, in July, 1931. *The Cricketer* reported that 'having taken his wife and children to a seaside bungalow, and left them there for the night, he returned to an empty house where he was found later by a friend dead in bed. He had complained of feeling unwell, and it is believed he died of heart-failure.' He was 51, and might it not be conceivable that he would have lived longer but for the physical stress he, along with all other fast bowlers, endured over the years? Kotze's career and expiry had much in common with Tom Richardson's and Schofield Haigh's.

One of the greatest of fast bowling sensations took place in 1905 when Neville Knox, from Dulwich College, took 121 wickets for Surrey in his first full season of first-class cricket. He had an exceptionally long run, building up speed every inch of the way, and his speed of delivery put him in the highest rank of fast bowlers that the world had ever seen. Jack Hobbs, who played alongside him for Surrey but against him in Gentleman v Players matches, rated him (in 1934) the best fast bowler he ever saw—and he saw them all from early in the century, through Gregory and McDonald in the 1920s, to Larwood and Voce in the 1930s.

'Still a very young man,' *Wisden* wrote of Knox after his glorious introductory season, 'he once or twice during the summer found county cricket rather trying but in nearly all the matches he kept up his full pace.' There followed criticism of his long run.

In the brief career that ensued, Knox often played when not fully fit, and was universally admired for his courage and his resolution. Finally it cost him perhaps up to half a dozen years of top cricket when, aged 25, he developed an acute form of shin soreness and had to struggle against chronic lameness. All the same, he had given much to the game.

It was a delight for all but the facing batsman to see Knox, well over six feet tall, storming in from near deep mid-off, loose-limbed and eager, and hammering the ball in at such a pace that it often reared from a fairly full length. It was the kind of attack which might have bought him piles of wickets for England. Yet he played only twice in Test cricket, against South Africa in 1907, with modest success. It was in that other testing zone, the Gentlemen v Players matches, that he proved himself—if proof were needed. He took 12 for 183, seven clean bowled, in the 1906 match, which commemorated the first such contest one hundred years before and which was marked by Arthur Fielder's 10 for 90 in the Gentlemen's first innings (N. A. Knox at number 10 surviving the onslaught with six not out). Martyn once more kept wicket splendidly, standing up to the terrific pace of Knox and Brearley, his only extra protection one pair of gloves inside another.

It was said that several of the leading wicketkeepers could have stood over the stumps to the Kortrights, Knoxes and Brearleys, but Lilley and Herbert Strudwick—to consider only two—felt it more profitable to stand back and minimise the byes at the same time as having a better chance to hold snicks. Nevertheless, such exhibitions as Martyn's to the abovementioned three and MacGregor to Woods bring to mind the remark of the prizefighter, Jem Mace, to Ted Pooley, Surrey's wicketkeeper in the 1860s and 1870s: 'I would rather stand up against any man in England for an hour than take your place behind the wicket for five minutes. I heard that ball strike you as if it had hit a brick wall.'

On that occasion a ball had leapt from one of the wide cracks in the Lord's pitch and removed three of Pooley's teeth. In taking a return from a fieldsman at Brighton in 1871 Pooley had a finger broken. He first noticed it when blood began to run down the sleeve of his flannel jacket, and upon removing his glove he saw that the broken bone was protruding from the flesh. When 'Old Ebor' (A. W. Pullin) discovered Pooley in the Lambeth Workhouse in 1899 he described the old 'keeper's fists as 'mere lumps of deformity'.

Neville Knox, with Walter Lees firing them down from the other end, helped restore Surrey's pride in 1905 and 1906 during which seasons they took 545 Championship wickets between them. In 1906 J. N. Crawford made a sharp third prong with 111 wickets with his brisk medium-pace.

After that the comet began to burn itself out. Soon no more would little Strudwick, as he arrested the screeching ball which had flown past the batsman's head, hear the captain, Lord Dalmeny (later the Earl of Rosebery), say, 'Well bowled, Neville!' No more would Knox jar his shins on the heartless Oval ground until the pain chiselled a grimace across his fine open face. No more would the Ovalites settle expectantly in their seats as, fair hair flying, Knox bounded in with all the menace of a kangaroo.

Surrey were well served for fast bowling subsequently when Bill Hitch began to realise the potential spotted by Tom Hayward when he saw him playing in Cambridgeshire. Here was another bowler with an off-putting run-up—a spluttering approach punctuated by several hops, black belt holding his flannels up—and boundless enthusiasm, so necessary on the Oval wickets. His career extended from 1907 into the 1920s, when he left behind him 1398 wickets, several broken stumps, over 200 catches, many taken at short leg with tigerish instinct, and almost 8000 runs. He had played for England seven times, without marked success, touring Australia twice. But for many years afterwards he was fondly recalled by Surrey followers who had cherished his ebullience, his hits out of the ground, and his raw yet intense fast bowling which once sent a bail flying over 55 yards.

There were so many interesting fast bowlers around before the First World War, but none with a more fascinating background than Hesketh Vernon Hesketh Prichard, who first played for Hampshire in 1900. A. A. Thomson wrote of him in *Odd Men Out*: 'There is a lying legend that fast bowlers are creatures of limited intelligence. The whole of Prichard's life, from his schooldays onwards, was a vigorous denial of this.' He was a brilliant rifle-shot, an explorer, travel-writer, conservationist, and honoured and decorated soldier, training snipers. His books included a study of life in Haiti and a travelogue on Patagonia, as well as *Sniping in France*, a classic of its kind. He was, between expeditions, a skilled sniper of batsmen, and might well have risen to international honours if he had stayed in the game consistently, for he often unseated the champion batsmen of his day, and drew much attention in 1904 by overthrowing the first five Kent batsmen for four runs for MCC when the county needed a mere 131 runs for victory. They were all out for 97. In the Gentlemen v Players match at Lord's that year he almost drew sparks from the pitch, taking 5 for 80 and breaking a bone in Albert Knight's hand.

He died in 1922, aged 45, of a rare blood disease.

It is often forgotten that G. L. Jessop, cricket's greatest consistent power-hitter, was a tearaway bowler in his early days, and though he strongly disapproved of Bodyline in the 1930s, he bowled something not far removed from it in the 1890s. Gerald Brodribb, in his long and detailed biography of Jessop (*The Croucher*), recounted how he attacked so savagely with bumpers from round the wicket in the Varsity match of 1896 'that he not only broke a stump, but damaged several of the batsmen, especially Leveson Gower, and knocked out his own wicketkeeper.'

His ferocity gave rise to a limerick oft-quoted in Cambridge:

> *There was a young Fresher called Jessop*
> *Who was pitching 'em less up and less up,*
> *'Til one of the pros*
> *Got a blow on the nose*
> *And said: 'In a helmet I'll dress up.'*

There was a grisly variant on the last line: 'And a man with a mop cleared the mess up.'

The question of helmets was to arise at intervals in the years that followed, most famously when Patsy Hendren devised a curious form of headgear in the early 1930s after being struck on the head. Forty years after that the topic returned to conversation. By the end of the twentieth century crash-helmets could well be accepted without demur. It has happened in baseball, and Tony Greig, discounting the suggestion that it would encourage bowlers to bounce even more at the batsmen, expressed the belief before the start of the 1975 season that batsmen would have more confidence in playing the hook—one of the most dramatic shots in the game—and cricket would be the more spectacular for it.

Warwickshire had some good fast men before the Great War, Frank Foster, who led the county to its first Championship, in 1911, being one, and additionally chronicling the others in distinctive prose. Of Frank Field he wrote in *Cricketing Memories* that he 'was undoubtedly the *best* fast bowler between the years of 1908 and 1914, and perhaps you, dear reader, may realise this certain truth before you have finished reading this book—if you *do* finish it.'

Time and again Foster comes back to Field in this oddest of autobiographies. He described his 7 for 20 when he bowled Yorkshire out before lunch for 58 as one of the finest exhibitions of fast bowling he had ever seen—and he saw plenty. 'I have said that Frank Field was a lion-hearted bowler, and I reiterate that true statement, with the addition that Frank Field was, is today, and always will be, a lion-hearted man. He was a great bowler, but to me he was a far greater man.... Friendships like ours have no need of passing time. Having once loved, we always love, come what may.'

Such affection from his captain must have been a help to any bowler.

Harry Howell was another very brisk Warwickshire bowler, and he *did* play for England and tour Australia. But in Foster's opinion 'to compare Howell with Field is like comparing brass with gold'. Howell first appeared for Warwickshire in 1913, when the fast attack of Foster, Field, Jeeves and himself constituted one of the best fast batteries of all time (Percy Jeeves, after whom P. G. Wodehouse named his fictional butler and who was killed in the war, was thought by many to be the best all-rounder in England at the outbreak of hostilities). Bowling off a long run, with an easy action, Howell was one of those bowlers who never enjoyed much luck with slip catches, reminding us again of the importance of strong support by wicketkeeper and fieldsmen. His greatest day was probably when he took all ten Yorkshire wickets for 51 at Edgbaston in 1923, though his demolition of Hampshire, also on his home ground, a year later, has endured because of the visitors' fight back. They disintegrated for 15 (Howell 6 for 7, Calthorpe 4 for 4), but made 521 in the follow-on and eventually won by 155 runs!

Of them all, F. R. Foster himself stands supreme. Six feet tall, fast left-arm, with a high, fluid action, he swung the ball prodigiously from around the wicket, was exceedingly fast off the pitch, and claimed many of his wickets in the leg-trap of close catchers. He owed much, too, to his wicket-keeper, E. J. 'Tiger' Smith, who in 1976 was the world's oldest living Test cricketer at 90.

Of all the fast-bowling combinations England have sent to Australia perhaps none has been quite as successful as that of 1911–12. Then, against an Australian team which boasted Trumper, Hill, Armstrong, Bardsley, Ransford, Minnett, and Kelleway, Foster took 32 wickets at 21·62 (eighteen bowled) and S. F. Barnes 34 at 22·88. With Hobbs, Rhodes, Woolley, Gunn and 'Young Jack' Hearne averaging between 35 and 82, and Johnny Douglas backing up the attack with fifteen low-cost wickets, England stormed to four comfortable victories after losing the first Test at Sydney. It was here that Douglas, who took over the captaincy after 'Plum' Warner had fallen ill, opened the bowling with Foster despite having Barnes in the side. After words from Barnes and the bedridden MCC captain (delivered in strikingly different tones) Douglas satisfied himself with coming on first-change thereafter.

In the second Test, at Melbourne, Barnes began the match with one of the most spectacular spells ever recorded, having overcome a bout of 'flu the night before by sweating under extra blankets, a bottle of whisky at his bedside. It may have left him weakened, but the Australians didn't notice. Bardsley (0) was bowled off his pads, Hill (4) was clean bowled by a ball which changed direction twice, Kelleway (2) was leg-before, and Armstrong (4) was caught behind by Smith. Australia 11 for four wickets; Barnes four for one. By lunch he had four wickets for three runs off nine overs, and after the interval Foster bowled Trumper (13) with a beauty and Barnes had Minnett (who was missed off him at third slip before scoring) caught by Jack Hobbs at cover for two. Australia now 38 for six, Barnes 5 for 6.

Australia struggled up to 184, with Hordern, the googly bowler, making 49 not out, and England, with centuries by Hearne and Hobbs, cruised to an eight-wicket victory,

Foster taking the figures in Australia's second innings with 6 for 91. But Barnes's first-morning performance was destined for the Oscar. Warner wrote: 'The present generation of Australian cricketers admitted that they had seen no finer bowling and the older men were equally enthusiastic. ... It was certainly one of the greatest feats, if not the very greatest, ever accomplished in a Test match and no Spofforth, or Palmer, or Richardson, or Lockwood, Lohmann or Turner could possibly have surpassed it.'

The combinations were irresistible. There was Barnes at one end, gaunt and war-like, veering and spinning the ball at fast-medium, with Foster at the other, offering nothing to the batsman but a flashing, oscillating red missile, and a fearless 'stumper' cutting almost everything off and presenting a constant threat to the straying back foot or the edged ball.

There was a little-known sidelight to 'Tiger' Smith's role behind the stumps, revealed entirely without malice in his old age by Herbert Strudwick, who kept wicket only in the first Test. He had always believed that Foster was anxious to have his own county 'keeper in the Test side, and when he signalled the little Surrey man to expect a leg-side delivery in the hope of a swift stumping chance, Strudwick moved to his left ... only to see the ball sail wide outside the off stump, to be taken by Woolley at first slip!

Foster, who had captained Warwickshire at only 22 years of age, was unquestionably an 'original'. He developed leg-theory bowling, with only three men needed on the off side, and he had his own way of handling men—as was hinted at in his appraisal of Frank Field. In addition to his leadership and his high-quality bowling, he was a splendid batsman, and his innings of 305 not out against Worcestershire at Dudley the year the world was plunged into war stands still as a Warwickshire record.

During the war years his cricketing life was ended suddenly, tragically, by a motor-cycle accident. He was only thirty when cricket resumed in 1919 and might well have had further seasons of all-round triumph. There were other sadnesses for him later in life, including, in 1950, his placing on probation for obtaining money by false pretences and credit by fraud. He died in 1958, in his seventieth year.

Foster bowled mainly at the leg stump, but looking back over the twenty years that preceded the Great War one sees a pattern of fast bowling on the line of the off, with the drive much in evidence and the manner of batsmen's downfall predominantly through slip catches, catches to the wicketkeeper, and to mid-off and mid-on. For years there was something dishonourable about bowling to leg. A bowler reckoned to concede the occasional cover-driven boundary and to tempt a catch through the off side. Either way the spectator enjoyed it. The Edwardian age slipped away, and with it went a kind of gaiety and insouciance that were never to be seen again in authentic form. Mankind was shaken by the four years of horror, and the jollity of the 1920s was founded on relief and bewilderment. It was reflected on the cricket field—not immediately, for there were traditions that had not died, but as a fresh generation developed its own kind of cricket to the dismal economic background of the early 1930s and the exciting introduction of other nations as they became Test match countries. The transformation was not as marked as that which took place in the twenty years following the Second World War, when the euphoria of the late 1940s gave way to the grim and negative cricket of the 1950s, which in turn ran on to the egalitarian 1960s and the slippery financial slopes of the 1970s.

One of the few things that have remained constant through the entire period from the start of the Golden Age in the mid-1890s until today has been the supply of fast bowlers. The county that has had two has invariably had success. The Test team in possession of one express bowler has had a head-start over its rivals: with two it has carried all before it. An outstanding example was Australia's attack immediately following the First World War. Before coming to them, there are other fast bowlers—some forgotten, some only partially forgotten—who galloped across the turf through the years when Queen Victoria, a wonderful, tired, old widow, came to the end of her long reign, and her son, Edward, gave the British and their Empire someone to exhilarate them and to speculate about in club, pub and parlour.

There was 'Bill' Bradley, an amateur for Kent, who had a resoundingly successful season in 1899, when he took 156 wickets at 19·10, including hat-tricks against Essex and Yorkshire, and 5 for 67 (off 33 overs) on his Test debut against Australia at Old Trafford. But Australia followed on compulsorily and Bradley bowled another 46 overs and was never quite the same force again. The same could probably be said of his fellow destroyer 'Sailor' Young, who bowled 37 overs in the second innings.

Bradley had stamina, and a preference for attacking the stumps, and his action was distinctive in that his long aggressive run-up culminated in both his arms being flung like a hoop high above his head, which was thrown back. He was later troubled by heart weakness, and died, aged 69, in 1944. He was buried a few yards from W. G. Grace's grave at Elmers End Cemetery.

Then there was William Beaumont Burns, who fell in action in France in 1916. He had exceptional speed, though his action was questioned, 'not without good reason' according to *Wisden*. There is no record of his having been called for throwing, but there were several instances of disgruntlement among opposing batsmen. He began his senior cricket with Staffordshire, and made many runs for them. In 1903 he assisted Worcestershire, and soon became a thousand-runs-a-year man. Indeed, he scored 196 against Warwickshire in 1909, adding 393 for the fifth wicket (still an English record) with Ted Arnold, who was a highly respected fast-medium bowler for Worcestershire and England whose praises Wilfred Rhodes, for one, never tired of singing.

By the time Burns settled in Canada in 1913 he had carved for himself a special niche as a purveyor of hot pace. He had bowled an Edwardian edition of Bodyline which had upset 'Plum' Warner considerably over twenty years before he was to find himself at the centre of the furore as MCC manager in Australia in 1932–33. Burns had made an impression as a bowler around 1908, when Ted Bale took over Worcestershire's wicketkeeping from the memorably-named Gaukrodger. Bale's job it was to take the thunderbolts of Burns and the bowling of R. D. Burrows, whose pace was not far behind. Standing up to Arnold, he earned his pay as have few wicketkeepers.

Burns toured New Zealand with MCC in 1906–07, and played for the Gentlemen against the Players twice in 1910 and at Lord's in 1911, taking 7 for 58, including three wickets in four balls, at The Oval in the first year. Whether his action was legitimate or not, he was now one of the most feared bowlers in cricket history, fast enough to deprive a batsman now and then of all his composure. His speed and belligerence—with Neville Knox bowling from the other end—were used by the Middlesex batsman Cyril Foley to illustrate his point that the so-called two-eyed stance, i.e. a turning forward of the right shoulder by the batsman as he awaits the ball, bringing more of his chest into view, was the chief cause of bowlers seeming to aim at the batsman's person. 'The bowler bowls at the batsman,' wrote Foley in *The Field*, 'for the very good reason that there is nothing else for him to bowl at. If the bowler happens to bowl short and fast the batsman says it is dangerous. So it is— damnably. But whose fault is that?'

A generous diagnosis from a former batsman.

Foley's story of his close shave against Knox and Burns went as follows: 'The wicket was rough, and I do believe that had I adopted the two-eyed stance I should have been killed twice and permanently injured four times, if you follow me. Balls grazing my eyebrows would have hit me in the eye; balls that hit me on the shoulder would have hit me on the heart; balls that hit me on the thigh would have hit me elsewhere, and so on.... In my humble opinion bowling at the batsman *in order to get him out* is a justifiable and unavoidable challenge to the two-eyed stance.'

Burns, who once scored a century and did the hat-trick in

a match against Gloucestershire, was lightning fast, if only for a few overs—what a Sydney Hill barracker might have called a 'milk bowler': the ball being pasteurised (past your eyes) before you see it! Yet if Burns was fast for a short spell, his partner in the Worcestershire XI, R. D. 'Dick' Burrows, was not only a bowler of sustained pace and marvellous reserves of stamina, but he went on and on until it was said that he was bowling as fast at the age of forty-one as in his prime. He played twenty seasons for Worcestershire, and was an awkward proposition when on target. Often, though, he was erratic, and this alone probably cost him an England cap. All the same, hundreds have played cricket for England, yet only one man has sent a bail as far as 67 yds 6 ins, and that was Burrows, at Old Trafford in 1911 when he bowled Bill Huddleston. Ten years earlier he had broken the wicket of the lordly MacLaren and dispatched a bail 64 yds 6 ins. Only Harold Larwood, apart from Burrows himself, has exceeded that, having sent a bail 66 yds in a match in Tasmania in 1928–29.

A massive man, with a black moustache, Burrows was also big in heart, offering his services as an amateur for the season of 1915 when Worcestershire fell on hard times. As it eventuated, of course, there was no cricket to speak of that season or for the following three.

'Plum' Warner, in his autobiography, *Long Innings*, wrote: 'When I first played for Middlesex in 1894 the stream of fast bowlers was at flood-level, and batsmen who disliked extra pace had to face it on every county ground. If you could not play fast bowling you might just as well give up any claim to batsmanship. Surrey had that incomparable pair Richardson and Lockwood, followed later by Knox and Hitch; Essex had Kortright and Pickett, followed by Buckenham; Kent had Bradley, followed by Fielder; Lancashire had Mold, followed by Brearley; Yorkshire had the great left-hander Hirst; Leicestershire had Woodcock, followed by Jayes and Skelding; Derbyshire had Porter, Warren and Bestwick; Warwickshire had Field; Sussex had Bland; Hampshire had Soar and Heseltine; Somerset had

Woods; Gloucestershire had Jessop; Worcestershire had Burrows and Burns; Nottinghamshire had Mee and, later, Wass, who was almost fast. Only my own county (Middlesex) had no regular fast bowler until Mignon in 1905, though Rawlin was medium-fast.'

The pad- and glove-making business should have been thriving, to say nothing of bone-setting medicos.

Three of the bowlers listed by Warner were to commit suicide, Woodcock by poisoning, Bland, at the age of 78, by trussing his hands and feet and throwing himself into a canal near Boston, and Pickett (presumably), his body being washed ashore at Aberavon several weeks after he was reported missing.

Harry Pickett was powerfully built, with sloping shoulders, and was a mainstay of the Essex attack for seventeen years to 1897. He bowled with a high arm and was regarded as above average in speed. He took what he described as the luckiest hat-trick on record: 'The first ball got Shilton caught, but the catch was taken so low down that only the umpire knew whether the man was out or not. I bowled Joe Creswell with the next ball, and then Harry Pallett received the third. It was not straight, and would not have bowled him, but it knocked his legs from under him and as he fell he trod on his wicket.'

His greatest performance came at Leyton on Spring Bank Holiday, 1895, when he took all ten Leicestershire wickets for 32. Kortright took 8 for 63 in the second innings, and curiously Arthur Woodcock took 12 for 115 in the match for Leicestershire. Woodcock, who took a long run and plunged all of his fine physique into his action, was considered for a season or two to be second only to Kortright in speed. He had helped the young Tom Richardson in his early days, when they both played at Mitcham, but later Woodcock took a position as coach to Haverford College in America, coming back to play for Leicestershire during the summer. His speed was such that in a minor match, for MCC against Lewes Priory at the Dripping Pan ground in 1908, he bowled a batsman and sent a bail an almost unbelievable 149½ ft, its carry taking it over a 14 ft bank and wall on the boundary. He was then 42. *Cricket* described his tragic end: 'Woodcock returned to his home at Billesdon late on Saturday night and asked his sister to kiss him, saying that he had come home to die. Shortly afterwards he became unconscious, and, although the doctors did everything possible to save his life, he passed away at three o'clock on Sunday morning.'

Cyril Bland, Sussex's Lincolnshire-born fast bowler, who took 543 wickets for the county between 1897 and 1904, had two claims to fame. His first wicket in first-class cricket was the best of all—W. G. Grace's—and he was the first Sussex bowler to take all ten wickets in an innings—10 for 48 against Kent at Tonbridge in 1899 (fast-medium bowler Ian Thomson became the second for the county when he took 10 for 49 against Warwickshire at Worthing in 1964). Bland rose to senior cricket through the Hertfordshire XI and in the Yorkshire leagues, and at one stage was hailed as some kind of new Tom Richardson. But he lacked the stamina and consistency, and it was said of him, as of others, that the increase in the amount of first-class cricket played was a discouragement to fast bowling when accurate medium-pace paid dividends and took less out of a man.

Claude Buckenham, who carried on the line of Essex fast bowlers, had the sad distinction of being one of those bowlers who continually suffer more than their fair share of dropped catches. Nevertheless, between 1899 and 1914 he took almost a thousand wickets for Essex, even if the cost was as high as 26·36. Tall, sparely-built, and with a toothbrush moustache, Buckenham used his height well to gain lift off the pitch. The 1909 season saw him at his best, when he took 6 for 98 for MCC against Noble's Australian team, and that winter he went to South Africa and played in his only four Test matches, taking 21 wickets at 28 apiece.

Another Essex fast bowler who might, given his due, have played more often for England was Harding Isaac 'Sailor' Young, who took twelve wickets, including Trumper twice, in his two Test matches in 1899. He was tall and raw-boned, with arms that seemed to hang almost to his knees, and his fast left-arm bowling round the wicket, given the right conditions, could be unmistakably vicious. He was almost unplayable for Essex against Darling's Australians in 1899, taking 4 for 42 and 7 for 32 in the county's victory, bringing the ball back six or eight inches at a rare pace. Young's nickname derived from the days when he was a serving sailor, and it was his form at the nets at Leyton that prompted C. E. Green to buy him out of the Royal Navy and take him on to the Essex staff. The county never had cause to regret their enterprise. By placing him in the hands of Bobby Peel, the great Yorkshire and England left-arm bowler, they ensured that he became aware of all the skills open to bowlers. The movement he imparted to the ball and the clever pace changes were good testimony to his intelligence in absorbing Peel's art.

Young became a first-class umpire when his playing days were over, and died in 1964, almost unnoticed, at the age of 88.

Arthur Fielder, who played for England six times, but only on tour in Australia—without distinction in 1903–04 but sharing the bowling success with Crawford and Barnes four years later—was Kent's spearhead for a dozen years before the Great War, his 158 wickets at 19.74 helping them to their first County Championship, in 1906, and was the only bowler in the long history of Gentlemen v Players —which terminated in 1962 when amateur status was abolished—to take all ten wickets in an innings. This was also in 1906, and his victims that July day at Lord's, on a damp wicket, were Spooner, H. K. Foster, Perrin, Jackson, Bosanquet, Hutchings, Crawford, Jessop, Martyn, and Brearley. He took four more wickets in the second innings, yet the Gentlemen won by 45 runs.

Fielder could move the ball either way, and his outswinger was additionally lethal in that he had some of the best slips fieldsmen in the country at his disposal—Mason, Hutchings, Woolley, Seymour—and a fine wicketkeeper (were Kent ever without one?) in Huish. Specialist bowlers have always gained sweet satisfaction from making runs, and one of the outstanding instances occurred at Stourbridge in 1909 when Kent were 320 for 9. Fielder came in, last man, to join Frank Woolley, and the pair added 235 for the tenth wicket—still an English record—Woolley 185 and Fielder an amazing 112 not out. It was something else with which to regale the boys at Rugby School in the years that followed, when Fielder coached there.

Kent were not to have a fast bowler of Fielder's class for over thirty years. P. E. Morfee, a Scot, was given a trial in 1910, but apart from bowling 'Plum' Warner for a 'pair' at Lord's, he achieved little, and moved on to the leagues. Only Lord Cornwallis, whose fitness was inconsistent, bowled genuinely fast for Kent in the post-Fielder years.

Derbyshire have seldom been without a high-quality fast bowler or two. As with several of the northern counties, the legend has it that club officials have had only to stand at the pithead and announce the need of a fast bowler and up comes a coal-encrusted able-bodied volunteer.

Frank Shacklock was an early asset to the county. He sometimes bowled round the wicket, with a slinging action, at a pace the old-timers would have called 'ripping'. He made the ball swerve from leg, and varied this with a fast off-break, and apart from taking four wickets with consecutive balls against Somerset in 1893 (for Nottinghamshire, whom he joined after a couple of seasons with Derbyshire), he took eight wickets in an innings five times, including an 8 for 45 against Yorkshire at Derby in 1885. Conan Doyle based the name of his detective, Sherlock Holmes, on Shacklock after batting successfully against him. At the end of his athleticism he emigrated to New Zealand, where he coached, and died in 1937, aged 75.

Arnold Warren, had he come from a more fashionable county, might have played more than once for England. As it was, he took 5 for 57 and 1 for 56 (Trumper twice— for 8 and 0) at Leeds in his one Test appearance. He had a 'rotary' action and held the ball at his fingertips, gaining a snappy break back from the off. His problem was inconsistency : one day he looked a world-beater, the next merely a workaday bowler. This may have had something to do with his fondness for a glass of beer. The Derbyshire Centenary Year Book (1970) refers to a match at Ashby-de-la-Zouch in 1912 when Warren 'emerged from the refreshment tent in which he had spent the duration of the luncheon interval to bowl as a man inspired and take seven Leicestershire wickets to bring victory to his side when it did not seem possible.'

He was another bowler to inscribe his name on the batting records, scoring 123 (though lame) against Warwickshire at Blackwell in 1910 and sharing a (still) world-record ninth-wicket partnership of 283 with his captain, John Chapman. It took them a mere 175 minutes, and came when, with two wickets standing, Derbyshire were still 111 runs short of avoiding an innings defeat.

Bill Bestwick was a miner, heavily-built, with endless reserves of energy and a resistance to age that saw him taking 10 for 40 against Glamorgan at Cardiff when aged 45. He began with Derbyshire in 1898, played his last match for them in 1925, and enjoyed his best season in 1921. Later he became an umpire, standing in Test matches, in one of which Don Bradman scored his then-record 334. Bestwick's career was not, however, a steady succession of faithful performances. In 1909 Derbyshire found it necessary to dismiss him for 'intemperance'. Indeed, for some time it had been their custom to appoint one of the players as a kind of guardian to Bestwick during away matches lest he lose himself in drink. He had once been faced with and acquitted of a charge following the death of a man in a pub brawl.

During the Depression of the late 1920s cricket became an even more attractive proposition for a working man with the right physical assets. Such a one was Bill Copson, who played his first cricket at the age of 17 during spells of unemployment during and following the General Strike of 1926. From Colliery team he progressed to Clay Cross in the Derbyshire League and thence to the county side itself, having drawn attention to himself by taking 10 for 5 in a league match. With his first ball in first-class cricket he dismissed Surrey's Andy Sandham, and during the years that followed he was usually among the wickets, except when back trouble held him up. His 160 wickets in 1936 contributed much towards Derbyshire's one and only Championship, and the next year he took 8 for 11 against Warwickshire, including four wickets in four balls. He toured Australia in 1936–37 but did not play in a Test; his three appearances for England were in 1939 and 1947. He also donned the umpire's coat at the end of his playing days. Others followed: Pope, Gladwin, Les Jackson, Rhodes, Brian Jackson, Alan Ward, Hendrick. The Derbyshire tradition of fast bowlers has shown no sign of wavering in the 1970s, even if the county's general fortunes were in shadow.

Looking back to the late-Victorian era, perhaps there was no more curious career than that of Frank 'Nutty' Martin, who played for Kent between 1885 and 1899. He was called up for England in 1890 for the Oval Test against Australia when Peel and Briggs were unavailable. By no means an express bowler, Martin, with his medium-pace left-armers, took 6 for 50 and 6 for 52. That was it. No more Tests except for the one at Cape Town played by Walter Read's side, when Martin took 2 for 39, and Ferris—now playing for England—pocketed 13 for 91 in the match. Murdoch, the former Australian captain, also played for England, while Frank Hearne, who played for South Africa in this match, had played for England three years previously.

J. W. Sharpe was another to win England colours less often than he might have expected. He began with Notts Colts but made his name with Surrey, taking 179 wickets in 1890, the year of his one home appearance for England, at The Oval, when Martin and Lohmann did most of the bowling. Jack Sharpe, who was handicapped by the loss of his right eye and always looked away from the camera, had a destructive yorker and snapped the ball back from the off even on hard pitches. He toured Australia with W. G. Grace's side in 1891–92, and took 6 for 84 in the first innings of the Melbourne Test, but that turned out to be the high point of his career and by 1894 he was back with Notts, soon to slip into oblivion. He was slender and only 5 ft 7 ins, and his exertions probably burned him out several years before his thirtieth birthday.

George Thompson of Northamptonshire had no such problem. He was a huskily-built, shy country boy who grew up with his county's cricket and was the central character in Northamptonshire's rise to first-class status in 1905. A batsman of aggressive instinct, he placed his side's needs first and usually contained himself. As a fast and inexhaustible bowler he and medium-pacer Bill East carried the county's attack, taking 964 wickets between them in 91 matches between 1898 and 1904.

Tall, with a black moustache and piercing eyes, Thompson bowled with a high arm, finishing with a completely circular swing, his lips pursed in an O which he might have been willing upon a new batsman. He had at his command the yorker, without which no self-respecting bowler could enter the field of play, and he could bring the ball back from some distance outside off stump. Batsmen also found his length difficult to judge. He played in one Test against Australia in 1909, bowling only four overs, and in all five in the losing series in South Africa the following winter, taking 23 wickets, as did the lob-bowler Simpson-Hayward. The war, in which Thompson was wounded, undoubtedly blocked his way to further successes, and after 1922 he became a coach at three Public Schools in turn. While the rest of the world may have forgotten him, Northamptonshire remember G. J. Thompson by a plaque on the pavilion.

Nor should the period be passed without mention of John Barton King, the Philadelphian, who holds an unchallengeable place as the finest of American-born cricketers. He was a superb batsman (still holding the North American record with 344 in a Halifax Cup match in 1906) but is best remembered for his bowling, which was very fast and based upon swerve which he cultivated as a baseball pitcher. He toured England with the Philadelphians in 1897, 1903, and 1908, taking 72 wickets at 24·20, 93 at 14·91, and 87 at 11·01 (the best in England that season). On the first tour he took 7 for 13 against Sussex, bowling Ranjitsinhji for nought first ball; on the second tour he took 5 for 46 and 9 for 62 (eight bowled) against Lancashire. So often he was the star of the annual USA v Canada match.

'Bart' King learned much from a succession of visiting teams to America during the 1890s, and had command of both the late inswinger and outswinger, the former being affectionately referred to as his 'angler'—a ball he could deliver at will preferably with a new ball but quite dependably and almost as deadly with a used ball. 'I liked best a following wind just enough to flutter the left corner of my shirt collar,' he wrote in *A Century of Philadelphia Cricket*. 'The fundamental essential I found to be complete relaxation and coordination—an absence of any tension in arms, legs, or shoulders. This was necessary because my angler required a whole-souled follow-through of body and arm that would carry me well on down the wicket. When conditions were favourable I had the feeling that I was hurling myself after the ball toward the wicket.'

He must have been one of the most intellectual of fast bowlers, analysing the techniques of himself and others, incorporating this, discarding that. He knew that the 'round-house' ('banana ball') was of limited potency since it announced itself early in flight; he was aware that baseball pitchers had refined it many years previously to the 'hook', i.e. a ball which stores up its swing until the final few feet. Even with his ability to swing the ball either way—and fatefully late—he knew the wisdom of interspersing a straight ball. He made a batsman's life a succession of problems, and the imagination seethes at the thought of what he might have achieved had he played regular county and Test cricket.

John A. Lester vividly described the balding King's appearance: 'Nature endowed this man completely with the physical equipment that a fast bowler covets. He stood six feet one inch, weighed 178 pounds, and never in his life has carried superfluous flesh. The physical characteristic that impressed Bart's friends most deeply, however, was not his powerful shoulders or the long and loosely hung arms and lean hips. It was rather the power in the wrists and fingers. This hand power had been developed and was maintained by special exercises of his own. With his wrist held tight Bart could send a new cricket ball to the second storey window with a snip of two fingers and a thumb.'

King was the subject of many an anecdote, the best known being his humiliation of the Trenton captain. King's club, Belmont, had decimated Trenton when the captain, who had arrived late, came to the crease muttering that his team would not be in such a mess if he had not been delayed. King promptly sent all his fieldsmen from the field, followed by the wicketkeeper. Then as an afterthought he called one fieldsman back and placed him precisely twenty yards behind the stumps and four yards to leg. He bowled his 'angler', hit the leg stump, and the lone fieldsman collected the ball as it ran through without having to move a pace.

On board ship returning from England he once responded to an amateur hypnotist's boast that he could lay anyone low if he chose by swaying, collapsing, and frothing at the the mouth. After a doctor, who was in on the act, had declared King dead, the frenzied little hypnotist was clapped in irons, and was rescued only by King himself, who, joke over, went below and exposed the ruse.

At Haverford in 1909 he bowled all eleven of the Irish Gentlemen in an innings—G. A. Morrow, who ended up as the not-out batsman, with a no-ball. This, like the man himself, remains distinctly unique. Bart King died in a Philadelphia nursing home, at the grand age of 92, in 1965, by which time the inswinger was commonplace, even if rarely bowled with the skill and shocking suddenness of King, the other 'Demon'.

9. TIME OF ENGLISH TERROR

Jack Gregory—Ted McDonald—England's 1921 problems

Gregory and McDonald! Upon English batsmen of the early 1920s this expression had the same chilling effect as Lindwall and Miller thirty years later and Lillee and Thomson twenty years after that. They bowled as a pair and in contrast; they complemented each other; and there was no relief until one or both tired. Gregory was 6 ft 3½ ins, fourteen stone, all massive arms and legs, with a run-up of only fifteen yards culminating in a huge kangaroo leap, and he could swing the ball out off a full length or bounce it up at the batsman's throat or over his skull when he dropped it just short of a length from his great height. He also happened to be the most spectacular slips fieldsman of them all, sometimes even taking catches across at leg slip, and his left-handed batting brought him runs swiftly and thunderously. The fastest Test century ever made stands to his credit: a 70-minute marvel against South Africa at Johannesburg on the way back from the 1921 tour of England.

McDonald, born in Tasmania, reached international cricket through the Victorian ranks, and was altogether more stealthy and sinister. In contrast to Gregory's crashing approach to the wicket, McDonald's run of around 20 yards was practically silent, and his action was smooth as silk. It was said he might have been bowling in carpet slippers.

Gregory, having captained his school XI and played lower-grade cricket in Sydney, was discovered by the organisers of the Australian Imperial Forces XI at the end of the First World War, when he was one of a great many soldiers in England awaiting return to their homeland. He had been in the artillery, but henceforth he was to pass the time bombarding batsmen. In that very summer of 1919 he blasted out 131 batsmen in matches against the counties and other sides, and remains, by the chance of having begun his first-class cricket in England, the only Australian to take 100 wickets in his debut summer. Chance played its part here—though his powers would have asserted themselves sooner or later—when Cyril Docker, who was originally regarded as the key fast bowler, strained his back, opening the way for Gregory. Gregory also found himself fielding at slip unexpectedly after damaging a finger in an outfield tumble. Herbie Collins thought this the best place for a man with a bad hand, and there Gregory stayed throughout his career, taking 44 catches in 1919 for a start.

Wisden attempted to classify him by stating that 'many batsmen who revel in ordinary fast bowling are uncomfortable against abnormal pace and that is what they got when they faced Gregory. He was very fast indeed—quicker than anyone else who bowled last summer—and helped by his great height and high delivery he often made the ball get up on the hard wickets in a way that reminded one of Knox in 1906. If he can resist the fascination of batting—he made two hundreds in one game when the team reached home after their victories in South Africa—he may be a great force in the Test matches of the future.'

He became very much of a force in the very near future. In the 1920–21 series against England, the first after the war, he was third in Australia's batting (442 runs at 73·66) and bowling (23 wickets at 24·17), and he took fifteen catches, a series record for a non-wicketkeeper which still stands. He hit 100 in the second Test, 93 in the fifth, and three scores of seventy-odd, and in the course of two months his name had joined those of the world's greatest all-round cricketers of all time.

He first bowled opposite Ted McDonald in the third Test,

at Adelaide, but the Tasmanian's successes still lay some months away. In three Test matches against J. W. H. T. Douglas's team he managed only six wickets at 65.33, but for the moment Australians were unconcerned, since Warwick Armstrong's side had won all five Tests, and when the 1921 series in England began a few months later they won three more, to make it eight in a row. English despondency reached new depths.

In England, McDonald's Test figures were the better: 27 wickets at 24.74. Gregory took 19 at 29.05, and his batting slipped away. Yet as a combination they were the sternest of challenges to English manhood. County and Test batsmen fought against their apprehension, and as the Australians steamrollered their way around England, making mountains of runs and dismissing sides with the high-explosives of Gregory and McDonald backed by the teasing incendiaries of Mailey and Armstrong, the psychological pressures multiplied. While many casualties were not recorded, some were: Vallance Jupp's thumb was damaged in the match against Lionel Robinson's XI; P. R. Johnson, MCC's captain, suffered a badly bruised hand (Jack Durston cut Armstrong's eye during this match, and after taking eleven wickets was hailed as England's fast bowling answer to Australia); Ernest Tyldesley was struck in the face by a ball from McDonald in the first Test and was helped from the field, only to learn that he was out 'bowled'; Hubert Ashton, who made the first century off the tourists, for Cambridge University, had to retire after a blow on the hand; J. R. Barnes of Lancashire was hit on the head; Percy Perrin of Essex was disabled by a fast one in the stomach; during the last Test match play was held up while England's captain, the Hon. Lionel Tennyson, recovered from a blow on the heart.

Tennyson's courage was one of the features of the series. In the Lord's Test match he was drafted in at the last moment upon the recommendation of C. B. Fry, and made 74 not out, facing the fire of the Australians with nerves of asbestos. He finished 'black and blue all over' for his trouble, but some desperately-needed English pride was restored by this show of courage, as by Frank Woolley's wonderful double of 95 and 93.

The first Test was won by Australia by ten wickets by the second evening, this second Test by eight wickets, and the third—in which Jack Hobbs made his sole appearance during the series only to be struck down by appendicitis before he could bat—by 219 runs. Yet in this third encounter there was further courage to be admired, and again it was Tennyson's. He had now taken over the captaincy from Johnny Douglas, but in Australia's first innings he had the misfortune to split the webbing between his left thumb and forefinger in intercepting a drive from Charlie Marcartney. Sitting in the pavilion with three stitches in the wound, Tennyson watched his side collapse to 67 for 5 in reply to Australia's 407 before Douglas, the deposed captain, and the robust George Brown of Hampshire added 97. By the fall of the seventh wicket Tennyson had decided to bat. He had unusually strong wrists and arms and a large heart, and picking the lightest of his bats from his bag he marched out to play a one-handed innings of 63 in little more than an hour, with ten boundaries, which had the crowd wild with excitement. The follow-on was avoided, but not, alas for his heroism, defeat at the end. He scored 36 second time round, and even held a one-handed catch in Australia's second innings. England were three down with two to play, but some morsel of prestige was salvaged, and the remaining Tests were drawn with England marginally in command. Tennyson would not stay out of the headlines, declaring illegally on the first day of actual play during the Old Trafford Test. Armstrong, his opposite number, then proceeded to bowl his second consecutive over after play was resumed, and to bring shame upon his head at The Oval three weeks later by leaving his bowlers to manage themselves while he skulked in the outfield, bored and reading a newspaper that had blown past.

A catastrophic year for England, 1921, and largely the doing of Gregory and McDonald. In all matches they took 270 wickets between them at sixteen apiece, and in five

Tests England, in her despair, selected thirty players. Tennyson summed up his country's plight when he wrote, in his rambling and entertaining autobiography *From Verse to Worse*: 'I remember one amateur who played for England being so nervous that he could hardly hold his bat, while his knees were literally knocking together. I endeavoured to put some heart into him by a few timely words when I joined him at the wicket, but it was useless; his nerve was gone, and the first straight ball was enough for him.'

Australia's express bowlers, feeling their utter dominance, were not going to let up. The greater the discomfort at their bouncers the more they would bowl. They carried their terror to South Africa on the way home, though it was not until the last of the three Test matches that they managed to pull off a victory. The main interest centred on the second Test, where Gregory's world-record fastest Test century was oddly matched by Springbok Charlie Frank's 152 in almost nine hours. It was here that Jack Zulch, opening for South Africa, innocently asked Herbie Collins, who had taken over the Australian captaincy from Armstrong, if Ted McDonald was really fast. 'Fairly quick,' said the droll Collins, 'but he needs to warm up.' McDonald did warm up—*behind the pavilion before the innings began*. His second ball shattered Zulch's bat, sending a fragment into the stumps. The scorecard reads 'hit wkt b McDonald', but there was more to it than that.

McDonald played no more Test cricket after this series, but his torture of English batsmen was really only just beginning, for after playing Lancashire League cricket with Nelson he qualified to play for Lancashire, for whom between 1924 and 1931 he took over a thousand wickets. In 1925 alone he took 205 wickets, and when he took fifteen wickets against Kent at Old Trafford in 1928 Neville Cardus was moved to write of him: 'Whence does McDonald draw his terrible strength and velocity? His run to the wicket is so easy, so silent. He does not thunder over the earth like Gregory—like a bull at a gate. No; he runs along a sinister curve, lithe as a panther, his whole body moving like visible, dangerous music. A more beautiful action than McDonald's was never seen on a cricket field, or a more inimical. The man's whole being tells of the sinister destructive forces of nature—he is a satanic bowler, menacing but princely.'

R. C. Robertson-Glasgow read into McDonald's 'saturnine and mahogany-grim' features : 'He loved to be thought the "tough baby", and he fell into ways of life that somehow foreshadowed tragedy.' He was killed by a passing vehicle early on the morning of July 22, 1937, near Bolton, while standing on the road at the scene of an accident in which his car was involved.

It is natural that serious comparisons between McDonald and Gregory have continually been made down the years, and such conclusions as have been reached do little more than confirm that as a double attack their ferocity can never have been surpassed. Jack Hobbs felt that Gregory's approach, which must have resembled an elephant stampede, together with his high bounce, exaggerated the impression of great speed, while Patsy Hendren thought him clearly the deadliest of the many fast men he faced. Hobbs's famous partner, Herbert Sutcliffe, who faced Gregory in Tests and McDonald in county matches, favoured—if that is the word —Gregory, though Larwood he thought the fastest of all. Bert Oldfield, Australia's wicketkeeper, shared this view. V. W. C. Jupp estimated interestingly that at the start of the day Gregory worked up to the fiercer pace, but as evening approached McDonald was hitting the wicketkeeper's gloves harder.

Whatever their relative merits, they were a phenomenon, and often during the 1930s Australians were to lament their absence as they awaited worthy replacements.

Jack Morrison Gregory, a nephew of little Syd Gregory (who played 58 times for Australia between 1890 and 1912) went on playing for Australia, though the edge was lost from his speed. In the 1924–25 series, when Bert Oldfield's leg-side catching of Hobbs off Gregory at Sydney was as exciting as Carter's wide off-side catch of the same batsman at Melbourne off McDonald four years earlier, Gregory took

22 fairly expensive wickets. In England a year later he could manage only three wickets in the five Tests for 298 runs, and in 1928–29 came the final calamity when at Brisbane, in the first Test, after bowling with much of his old fire and stamina—indeed, one good-length ball had chipped a shoulder off Larwood's bat—he broke down with a recurrence of a knee cartilage injury, and sobbed the news to his team-mates that he was 'done for'. He did not play for his country again; he was 32.

In 24 Tests he took 85 wickets at 31·15 apiece and scored 1146 runs at 36·96; in first-class cricket he took 504 wickets at 20·99. The figures are not sensational. The man was. Heavily-built, small-headed, with hair slicked back, invariably capless, often batting gloveless, he was the darling of the Australian crowds in the 1920s and a symbol to English crowds of the Digger, the bronzed and husky Aussie. Ian Peebles was to remember him as the finest cricketer of them all, the one he would most like to see play if time could be manipulated like a videotape. Reg Perks, the Worcestershire and England opening bowler, recalled being coached by Gregory when he went to Hereford during the 1926 tour, determining from that day to model his final leap upon Gregory's.

He spent his last years in seclusion at Narooma, on the south coast of New South Wales, fishing and playing bowls. His wife, a former Miss Australia, died in 1963, and he lived alone for the remaining ten years of his life. That knee, which had taken such a pounding in his Test match days, was still acting as a barometer, swelling up when rain was on its way, and the abiding smell in the cottage was of liniment. He died in 1973, one week short of his 78th birthday.

10. SPEED AT HOME AND ABROAD

Maurice Tate—Arthur Gilligan—George Geary
Mahomed Nissar—Indian dearth—Allom's hat-trick
George John—Learie Constantine

England's quest for a genuinely fast bowler was to go on for some years after the resumption of play following the First World War, just as it went on after the Second, until the advent of Trueman. Batting—professional batting—ruled the day, with Hobbs, Woolley, Hendren, Sutcliffe, Sandham, Mead, Ernest Tyldesley, Hearne, Dipper, Holmes, Makepeace, George Gunn, Hallows, and, soon, Hammond heading a solid phallanx of paid run-getters who batted on pitches usually over-prepared with fine marl, manure and assorted cosmetics, and with outfields barer than those in modern times, when fertilisers have turned the county grounds a lush green and kept the ball an insistently gleaming red. The old pro looks at the fast bowler of the 1970s and despises him for the crimson smears defacing the groin of his flannels. In the old days a quick wipe on the shirt-sleeve sufficed.

There was relief in store for the bowler. In 1927 the ball was reduced in size from between nine and nine and a quarter inches in circumference to between eight and thirteen sixteenths and nine inches. Four years later the size of the wicket was increased to 28 inches by nine. Perhaps for a time the balance seemed to have been restored, but never have exponents of all departments of the game been satisfied unanimously that playing regulations are completely just.

The custom of opening the bowling with a fast and a slow bowler at opposite ends was dying. W. G. Grace may have proclaimed that nothing gets a man's eye in better than two fast bowlers on a plumb wicket, but it was now recognised that with a respectable fast man at each end, a swinging ball, and a slips field to go with it, the best results might reasonably be expected. There were still instances of slow bowlers taking one end at the start of an innings—Dick Tyldesley for Lancashire, Charlie Parker for Gloucestershire—but the age of the dual-hunters had dawned. Hampshire had their Kennedy and Newman, who took almost five-thousand wickets between them; Yorkshire had Emmott Robinson and George Macaulay, with Waddington a third agent; Middlesex had Haig and Durston, with Gubby Allen rising; Worcestershire had Fred Root, the inswinger with the crowded leg-side field, and Pearson; Essex had Louden and Johnny Douglas; Leicestershire had Skelding and Geary; Derbyshire had Bestwick and Cadman; and Sussex —Sussex by the sea, with its fret and encouragement to opening bowlers—had their Tate and Gilligan.

Maurice Tate and Arthur Gilligan were not just Brighton's favourites. They bowled for England. Tate (whose father, Fred, had played once for his country in 1902, dropping a catch and being bowled out, last man, when England were three runs short of Australia) started as a successful hard-hitting batsman and off-break bowler, but abandoned this bowling after several seasons when he found he could bowl a fast leg-cutter. Phil Mead was the first dismissed by it, and hundreds followed. An immense man, with a cherubic face and hearty sense of humour, Tate was a natural bowler, with broad hips, heavy shoulders, huge feet. He operated off a run of only about eight yards, and leant back at the start of his swing, bringing his right arm over with the full momentum of his great body. No-one in the history of the game has given a more distinct impression of 'making pace off the pitch'—a scientific impossibility, but a cricketer's way of saying that the ball lost less of its pace than usual upon impact with the pitch. The ball appeared to dive from its height and more often than not swerved late from leg, resulting in many 'clean bowleds' from 'unplayable' balls and even more narrow misses, the wicketkeeper throwing his head back in astonishment. He may not rate as one of the fastest of bowlers, but the fact remains that Tate's slip fieldsmen, particularly in Australia, stood much deeper than to any run-of-the-mill medium-pacer.

He played 39 times for England—twenty times consecutively against Australia—between 1924 and 1935, taking 155 wickets at 26·13, and in all first-class cricket he dismissed 2784 batsmen at an average of 18·12. One of his records which has withstood challenge is his 38 wickets in the Tests in Australia in 1924–25. Only four bowlers have taken more wickets in a series anywhere, and Laker's 46 and Bedser's 39, both against Australia, were taken in England.

Ian Peebles, who played against and with Tate, rated him the greatest exponent of pure seam bowling that the game has yet seen—this remark in 1965—and M. A. Noble, as shrewd a judge as cricket has known, described him as a 'shock merchant'. John Arlott, who admired him as no other, wrote: 'Bowling into the wind on a heavy seaside morning, he would make the ball dart and move in the air as if bewitched. The inswing and outswing were there as a matter of course but, as every man who batted against him at his best will testify, the ball would sometimes seem to begin to swerve and then straighten again before it struck the ground. Once it pitched, the bounce was full of fire and, because Tate was a "long-fingered" bowler, on a green-topped wicket the ball would sometimes strike back in the direction opposite to the swing.... The ball would whip into Tich Cornford's gloves with a villainous smack and the little man would hollow his belly and was lifted to, or off, his toes as the ball carried his heavy-gloved hands back into him.'

His batting was good enough to bring him over 17,000 runs for Sussex, a century for England against South Africa at Lord's, and five centuries in the 1927 season. Further,

his stand of 385 with Ted Bowley against Northamptonshire at Hove in 1921 remains a Sussex second-wicket record. Yet all this tends to be overlooked because of his
tremendous stature as a bowler. The performance by which
he may be best remembered was in his first Test match,
against South Africa at Edgbaston in 1924. He began with
a wicket, Susskind, first ball, and finished with 4 for 12. His
county partner and skipper, Arthur Gilligan, took 6 for 7
from the other end, and the tourists were put out for 30,
of which 11 were extras. Following on, South Africa made
390 on a pitch and in an atmosphere less conducive to seam-
bowling, but still lost by an innings. The Sussex pair took all
nineteen wickets that fell to bowlers.

It seemed that England had as effective an opening pair
as could be wished for, but later that summer Gilligan was
knocked out by a blow under the heart from a ball from
'Dick' Pearson during the Gentlemen v Players match at The
Oval, and was never the same force again. He might not
have been weakened permanently had he refrained from
batting in the second innings, but he went to the crease in
the follow-on, and moreover scored 112, one of several
centuries he made batting from number six to eleven—a
unique record.

A. E. R. Gilligan captained England in Australia that
winter, 1924–25, losing the series 4–1. Observers felt it
would have been appreciably closer had he been able to
bowl with the speed and stamina so often shown before his
accident.

He had first shown his capabilities while at Dulwich College, and in the 1919 University match, in taking 5 for 16
for Cambridge on the last morning, he drew comparison
with the Repton fast bowler, A. F. Morcom, who had done
great things for Cambridge in 1905 and 1907. He was then
bowling inexhaustibly, specialising in the deadly outswinger
of which Tate was also master. In those glorious days in the
field for Sussex in the early 1920s the off stump took a
battering and the slips and wicketkeeper were kept busy.

His playing days behind him, his Test career effectively

Mike Procter (b1946), the South African express who showed that great speed does not have to stem from a conventional action. His 'wrong-foot' delivery off a long-distance run-up perplexed purists and bamboozled batsmen. *(Patrick Eagar)*

John Snow (b1941) of Sussex and England, destroyer in his time of
Australia and West Indies, but victim of his moods. Self-styled
'Cricket Rebel'. *(Patrick Eagar)*

Evenining Standard

EATHER:
older,
ghting-up
p.m. to 6.24 a.m.
etails—Back Page.

London: Tuesday February 25 1975   5p

CITY PRICES

Paceman Peter Lever: I bowled short deliberately

I THOUGHT I'D KILLED HIM

says weeping Test star

PETER LEVER—"What I can't forget is that the ball was a deliberate short one."

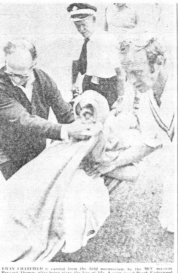

EWAN CHATFIELD is carried from the field unconscious by the MCC masseur Bernard Thomas after being given the kiss-of-life. A grim-faced Derek Underwood gives a helping hand.

How the news reached England of New Zealander Ewen Chatfield's brush with death after being struck by a ball from England fast bowler Peter Lever (b 1940) in the 1975 Auckland Test.

Top: Dennis Lillee (b 1949) not only took a record 31 wickets in the 1972 Test series in England – he established a mastery over Geoff Boycott, considered by many to have been the world's best batsman. *(Patrick Eagar)* *Bottom:* Asif Masood (b 1946), Pakistan's fluent and penetrative opening bowler. *(Patrick Eagar)*

Australia's Jeff Thomson (b 1950), the sensation of the 1974-75 series, when he took 33 wickets in five Tests. His classical slinging action, an enthralling sight – if not necessarily to taut batsmen – is captured here in one of the finest-ever sports photographs. *(Patrick Eagar)*

Dennis Lillee (b 1949) – a beautifully-controlled nineteen-pace approach which causes tremors in the stoutest batsman's heart. (*Patrick Eagar*)

Andy Roberts (b 1951), Hampshire's West Indian, has spread havoc
with his exceptional speed and lift. *(Patrick Eagar)*

Michael Holding – the sensational speed discovery of the 1976 West Indies v England Test series. *(Patrick Eagar)*

ended during the 1932–33 tour of Australia when England's captain D. R. Jardine saw no place for him in his blistering Bodyline attack, Maurice Tate became a publican and also coached at Tonbridge School. Arthur Gilligan remained close to the game as selector, writer, and broadcaster, and became president of MCC in 1968, always remembering fondly his huge fellow opener, who, let it never be forgotten, bowled more overs during the 1924–25 Tests than any other two England bowlers—with all his massive bulk coming down on a left foot and a big toe that were, after all, only flesh and bone. At one stage the toenail had been pushed inwards and turned the digit septic, and the doctors for a time feared that amputation would be necessary. But 'Chub' survived, continuing on his way with an oath always attended by a grin as a catch went down or a ball shaved the stumps. England was ever proud of him.

After the First World War Australia adopted the eight-ball over, which has never been popular with fast bowlers. Jack Gregory told Arthur Gilligan that he always held two balls back each over, i.e. 'coasted'; but there must have been a special skill in this, for the crowds soon let Gilligan know when they spotted him holding back, bowling slightly wide.

The longer over, the harder grounds, the intense heat and humidity—these have always been the supreme test of a bowler, especially the faster variety. And one of the finest exhibitions of courage and stamina came during the 1928–29 series, when George Geary, the Leicestershire fast-medium bowler, bowled 101 overs (six-ball overs were bowled in this series) in the final Test, at Melbourne, 81 in the first innings, when he took 5 for 105. He headed England's bowling averages in the series with 19 wickets at 25·10.

Geary played fourteen times for England, and was especially deadly on South Africa's matting wickets in 1927–28 before an elbow injury kept him out of the game. One of sixteen children of a bootmaker and his wife, he was bedevilled by injury more often than most, having been struck by an aeroplane propeller in the war, smashed in the nose by a ball from Western Australia's Ron Halcombe that reared from a length ('They carried me off on a door; they hadn't got a stretcher!'), and thrown out that arm in Cape Town. He bowled with an aggressive yet beautiful action, and cut rather than spun the ball, keeping a perfect length for over after over. In figures his grandest performance was 10 for 18 against Glamorgan at Pontypridd in 1929, but many times he took seven or more wickets in an innings. His leg-cutter—a ball upon which he later advised the young Alec Bedser—was lethal enough to upend any batsman in the world, and accounted for Don Bradman one afternoon at Leicester. Besides this gift for bowling, Geary was also a good enough batsman to make seven centuries for his county and another in the Gentlemen v Players of 1934, and had few peers as a slip fieldsman. In the famous Oval Test of 1926, when England regained the Ashes, he took two catches from the bowling of the young debutant Larwood that bruised *the back of his hand*.

He played, almost continuously, for Leicestershire from 1912 until 1938, and as a legacy for all his endeavours, in his old age his worn hip had to be replaced by one made of plastic. What gave him about as much satisfaction as anything else in his long and creditable career was his coaching of a schoolboy at Charterhouse—a lad for whom he predicted not just county honours but international: P. B. H. May.

Peter May grew into a batting master in an age—the 1950s—when cricket was more an international game than ever before. Seven countries were competing regularly in Test cricket. Yet until 1928 only England, Australia and South Africa had played Test matches. West Indies entered the ring—prematurely—in 1928, losing all three Tests in England by an innings; New Zealand entertained England for their first Tests in 1929–30; and India made the dizzy ascent with a solitary Test at Lord's in 1932. From those respective initiations until today it may be said, in simple terms, that West Indies have seldom lacked at least one fast bowler of real speed and danger, New Zealand have developed precious few of the species, and India none at all, apart from Mahomed Nissar and Amar Singh.

These two strapping men, supported by a competent collection of fieldsmen, made an impression during the 1932 tour, and kept India in the match for some little time during the maiden Test match. Nissar, faster than Larwood for a few overs according to his contemporary C. K. Nayudu, took 5 for 93 in England's first innings, which lurched at one point at 19 for 3. Two long innings by Jardine, supported by Ames and Paynter, ensured an England victory, though Amar Singh chipped in with India's top score of 51 in the last innings.

During the tour, Nissar took 71 wickets at 18·09, and Amar Singh, whom Wally Hammond considered 'as dangerous an opening bowler as I have ever seen, coming off the pitch like the crack of doom', took 111 wickets at 20·78. He took only a short run, but climaxed it with a sudden, almost frenzied, unorthodox action, bending the ball in or out, and always coming surprisingly fast off the turf. He died in 1940 aged only 30.

Nissar was also an intelligent bowler, taken to England in 1932 on the strength of some good performances in intercollegiate matches in Lahore, and returning in 1936 to take twelve wickets in the three Tests, including six good ones at The Oval.

From such promising beginnings it is sad to reflect on India's prolonged fast-bowling famine. The Indian climate and the pitches have never been conducive to this form of attack, the unfortunate side-effect being that few batsmen themselves have been confident against really fast bowling when they have met it at home or more particularly abroad. Among the men who have bowled the new ball for India since the last war are Divecha, Phadkar, 'Tiny' Desai, Abid Ali, Solkar, and Madan Lal. None of them has ever put an Occidental into fear for his physical safety. India's successes have been achieved through batting, smart fielding, and varied spin bowling. Prior to the selection of their team for the Prudential World Cup in 1975 there was hopeful talk about Pandurang Salgaonkar, the fastest Indian bowler seen for many years. But he did not gain selection.

Within a few hours of New Zealand's entry into Test cricket they must have doubted the wisdom of taking the step, for their first seven wickets fell for 21, and thanks chiefly to Roger Blunt's 45 not out they managed to drag themselves up to 112. The Christchurch wicket was fast, and the England side, led by Harold Gilligan (Arthur's brother) had Stan Nichols of Essex and Maurice Allom of Surrey as its opening bowlers. Nichols, a fast-medium right-arm bowler and powerful left-hand bat, swept away the first three wickets with two Duleepsinhji slip catches and a caught-and-bowled, then Allom, a very tall amateur recently down from Cambridge, bowled one of the most sensational overs in Test history.

The first ball hit Blunt on the foot and came close to having him lbw; the second cut back to knock Dempster's off stump back; the third beat Lowry without consequence; the fourth had him lbw; the fifth had James caught behind off the inside edge by Cornford, standing up; the sixth was a beautiful ball which clean bowled Badcock. Four wickets in five balls, including the hat-trick. Yet Allom was to play only four more times for England, three on this tour, during which New Zealand began to feel their way more confidently. In the next Test, at Wellington, Mills and Dempster posted 276 for the first wicket, still a record opening partnership by any country against England—this after the sinister pointer of two balls from Nichols which flew over Dempster's head in the first over of the match.

While this inaugural series was being played, another England side, under the Hon. F. S. G. Calthorpe, a tall, thin fastish swing bowler with a curved run-up, was taking on West Indies in the Caribbean, the four-match rubber finishing one-all, with England making 849 (Sandham 325) in the last Test, at Kingston, Hendren averaging 115.50, and George Headley scoring four centuries. This was the first showing of West Indies as a potential world cricket power,

contrasting strongly with their dismal showing in their inaugural Tests in England in 1928. For years Headley was to
carry their batting, but West Indies' particular asset was
recognised—and has continued to be recognised—as fast
bowling. It may be too obvious a conclusion that the Negro
has a physical advantage in these matters, but the fact remains that West Indies have never lacked a truly fast
bowler, or a pair, for very long.

In pre-Test match days there were men like Cumber-
batch, fast-medium, and 'Float' Woods (who named himself after Sammy Woods of Somerset), both of Trinidad.
'Plum' Warner considered Woods to be among the fastest
bowlers in the world, even though he bowled off only two
paces. His confidence depended upon his being able to 'feel
de pitch wid de toe', and unless he could sense the big toe
of his right foot against the turf he was lost. He abhorred
having to wear boots, and it troubled him that his captain,
H. B. G. Austin, insisted during the 1900 tour of England
that he should wear boots. It was said that he sometimes
left the field and secretly tore off the soles of his boots,
returning to bowl apparently properly clad but with the
uppers little more than spats.

Clifford Goodman, one of a talented Barbados brother-
hood, was a large coloured man who often had the measure
of the famous English batsmen who visited his island with
private touring teams just before the turn of the century.
He was also responsible for one of the earliest recorded
run-outs of a non-striker, creating the downfall of visiting
American batsman Etting for backing up prematurely during the 1887–88 tour.

In 1923 England saw George John and George Francis,
then rivalling Gregory and McDonald as destroyers even
though John was around 40 years of age, with his best years
behind him, vivid in memory to West Indian cricket fans,
who were virtually the only ones to have seen him at his
peak. John, from Trinidad, was 5 ft 10 ins, very strongly
built, and he bowled with a high arm, bringing the ball back
from the off. 'Many a poor batsman hit on the inside of

the knee collapsed like a felled ox,' wrote C. L. R. James of him in *Beyond a Boundary*. 'He had an intimidating habit of following down after the delivery if the ball was played behind the wicket. When his blood was really up he would be waiting to receive it only a few yards from you.... At the end of the day he strode back like a man just beginning. Before almost every ball he was rolling up his sleeves like a man about to commit some long-premeditated act of violence. He was not the captain of his side, but I never saw his captain take him off. John always took himself off.'

For years he was head groundsman at Queen's Park Oval, Port of Spain. His son, Errol, became an actor and prize-winning playwright.

John's 49 first-class wickets at 19.51 put him second in the West Indians' bowling on the 1923 tour of England; top was George Francis, who, unemotional, undemonstrative, bowled as straight as he could at a sharp pace and took 82 wickets at only 15.58. Third in the bowling was another fast man—and one of the most exciting all-round cricketers the world has seen—Learie Constantine. 'Connie' was an unexcelled hitter, though not as reliable as Jessop, a fields-man for whom the description 'brilliant' is almost faint praise, and a tearaway fast bowler who, with Francis and Herman Griffith, formed a dynamic trio which was later transformed into the even more paralysing attack of Martindale, Hylton and Constantine.

Constantine was the son of a plantation foreman who was one of Trinidad's favourite cricketers, and he soon perceived the opportunity which cricket afforded an un-privileged black West Indian to improve his lot. He became the first coloured professional to play in the Lancashire League, joining Nelson, who won the competition eight times in his ten seasons with them. In time he was to be-come a barrister, MP in Trinidad, Minister of Works, High Commissioner in London, a knight, and ultimately a peer. At his death in 1971, at the age of 68, he was remembered for many things—not least his work in race relations—but to cricketers he remained a player from whom sparks flew.

At Georgetown in 1930, when West Indies won a Test match for the first time, he took 4 for 35 and 5 for 87, bowling at a fierce pace accentuated by the wicket, which was harder and faster than any he ever found in England. In the first Test of that 1929–30 series, in Barbados, he presented a fearful sight to an England XI many of whom were far beyond the first flush of youth. Teeth flashing, he bounded in and bowled bouncer after bouncer, with only two men on the off side—a forerunner of Bodyline. Andy Sandham made a highly creditable 152, Hendren, hooking valiantly, 80, and George Gunn, then having turned fifty, made 35 as opener, adopting tactics all his own: to Constantine he advanced down the pitch before the ball was bowled and played the short deliveries with a dead bat shoulder-high. This infuriated the bowler, who then began to run through in an attempt to bring off a caught-and-bowled. At this, Gunn would kill the ball, blow the bowler a raspberry, and skip back to his crease. The situation exploded eventually when the batsman was hit painfully under the armpit.

R. E. S. Wyatt has written of Constantine's aggression during the West Indians' match against Warwickshire in 1928. As Wyatt went out to bat he passed the unconscious form of Bates, the preceding batsman, who was being carried off after a bouncer had felled him. The first two balls Wyatt received from Constantine glanced off his head for four, and it was left to J. H. Parsons to push back the tide with an aggressive bat that brought him 161 runs.

Constantine was in on the climax of West Indies' second Test victory too. It was played at Port of Spain, the second Test of the 1934–35 series, and in the last over Leyland was faced with the prospect of holding up England's last wicket. He fell lbw to Constantine, giving the home side victory by 217 runs. Earlier, Constantine had been warned for bowling Bodyline and after a complaint by the umpire, Arthur Richardson, the former Australian Test player, he was taken off by his captain, G. C. Grant. It would have been better for England's cause if he had stayed off.

E. A. 'Manny' Martindale was a small man, a Barbadian,

who took 37 wickets in ten Tests at 21·72, and had a number of successful seasons in the Leagues. Perhaps the most significant ball he ever bowled was that which split Hammond's chin in the Old Trafford Test of 1933, when he and Constantine bowled, at their captain's instruction, a form of Bodyline which showed many who had not appreciated the fact that fast, short-pitched bowling towards the batsman's body with an accompanying arc of leg-side fieldsmen was neither cricket nor entertainment for any but the ghoulish. Hammond stated firmly that if that was what Test cricket had come to, he had had enough of it.

Another member of West Indies' notorious pre-war fast bowling battery was Leslie Hylton, a Jamaican, who played an important part in the 1934–35 rubber and toured England in 1939, by which time a little of his fire had subsided. He was hanged in Jamaica in 1955 for the murder of his wife.

Barbados has long had a tradition of producing world-class fast bowlers, and one of the best of the pre-war crop was Herman Griffith—a surname to have resounding echoes thirty years later. H. C. Griffith was short and thickly-built, cocky, and bowled a decidedly fast ball which usually swung outwards late. He was thought unlucky to miss selection for the 1923 tour of England, but finished second to Constantine in the tour bowling averages of 1928. In 1933, by which time he was in his fortieth year, he was a failure. His mark had been made, however, during the 1930–31 tour of Australia, when he presented Don Bradman with his first duck in Test cricket. The wicket was damp in both Australia's innings, and Bradman came to the crease at a crucial stage in the second innings, in which the home side were striving after 251 runs for victory. Learie Constantine remembered Bradman's brief innings in his book *Cricket and I*: Griffith's first ball to the new batsman was fast, down the leg side, and Bradman refrained from playing at it, watching it go through to 'keeper Ivan Barrow; the next was outside off, and Bradman missed with a cut; now one on the stumps, which Bradman parried, followed by a nasty ball that cut back and smacked his thigh; the last ball, on middle stump, was played away. From the opposite end bowler and fields-men saw to it that Kippax was given no ready chance to steal the strike. Maiden over. Then Griffith resumed to Bradman, who was averaging 89 in the series. Another leg-side delivery was allowed past, as was a widish off-side ball, before a straight ball impelled the batsman to come out, swing with 'an almighty cross-bat swipe', to be bowled neck and crop. West Indies went on to record their first victory over Australia, by 30 runs, and were a step nearer full maturity.

One further moment of fascination remains to be glimpsed from that tour. During the match against Queens-land, Constantine hit the Aborigine fast bowler Eddie Gilbert for six over square leg. The little native came down the pitch and shook 'Connie's' hand, saying he had never been hit for six before in his life.

The names of these West Indians—and of Eddie Gilbert too—might have featured more strongly in discussion over the years intervening had it not been for the events of the Australian season of 1932–33, when a group of English cricketers perpetrated an infamous form of bowling attack which the authorities were compelled eventually to mark as illegal and which batsmen (of both sides) and spectators found detestable. They called it Bodyline.

11. ON THE LINE OF THE BODY

Bradman the target—bitter series—McCabe's heroism
Harold Larwood—legislation against intimidation—Bill Voce
Bill Bowes—Ken Farnes—Alf Gover—Tim Wall
Ernie McCormick—Bob Crisp—Jack Cowie

Bodyline bowling, referred to euphemistically and insistently by many of its advocates by the cleaner-sounding 'leg theory', was introduced principally to trump the phenomenal batsmanship of Don Bradman. The young Australian scored 2960 runs in 1930 on his first tour of England, with 974 runs in his seven innings in the Test matches. At Trent Bridge he made 131, at Lord's 254, at Headingley 334, at The Oval 232. England's desperation may readily be understood.

The idea that Bradman could be stopped—or at least steadied—came during the final Test of 1930, when, although he made 232, he seemed unusually put out by balls from Larwood and Hammond which flew from a reasonable length during a period of play when the pitch, after rain, harboured gremlins. Archie Jackson, with whom Bradman added a record 243 for the fourth wicket, got faithfully into line and was bruised on thigh, hip and elbow for his troubles. Once he was even struck on the jaw. The comparison between the attitudes of the two young New South Wales batsmen was absorbing—and was not lost on England's wicketkeeper, George Duckworth. Australia went on to win by an innings, but certain English cricketing heads were put together, and the outcome two years later was to leave cricket—and Anglo-Australian relations—atremble for years to come.

Douglas Jardine, Indian-born, Winchester and Oxford educated, was a haughty, intense, apparently humourless man, a dour batsman who had finished second to Hammond in the MCC batting averages for the previous tour in 1928–29. His appointment as captain for the 1932–33 tour was a guarantee that the on-the-field policy, once decided upon, would be carried out without a backwards or sideways glance and without interference from the team manager, 'Plum' Warner, or his assistant, Richard Palairet. Jardine had an extremely strong fast battery—Larwood, Voce, Bowes, Allen, Tate, Hammond—and he intended to use it to the limit. The limit in those days before a Law against intimidatory bowling happened to be flimsy—dependent really upon the conscience of a fast bowler and his captain.

Of the six bowlers named, Tate, now 37, was to play no part in the Tests, despite having shown a sharp edge in a preliminary match against New South Wales. Hammond, as one of the key batsmen, was used as a support bowler, and Gubby Allen, an amateur and Sydney-born, refused to bowl Bodyline. He took 21 wickets in the series, second to Larwood, but his greater contribution lay four years ahead, when he was charged with the job of leading MCC in Australia on the first post-Bodyline tour, when the moral wounds were still weeping.

England's heavy artillery, then, consisted of Larwood, left-handed Voce, and Bowes, all of whom were instructed to bowl at or even outside leg stump once the ball had lost its sheen and stopped swinging. The evil adjunct was a ring of close fieldsmen on the leg side and sentries posted on the leg boundary, for the hook and the top-edge. Batsmen were left with the choice of trusting the hook and hoping to find the boundary or playing defensively, with the high risk of feeding the legside cordon, or withdrawing the bat and taking the ball anywhere from the lower abdomen to the skull. Ponsford frequently turned his back and let the ball hit him on his ample backside or shoulders, once being bowled behind his legs by a ball from Voce which failed to rise as expected. This was at Adelaide, where he made a courageous 85 and reckoned his bruises were worth £2.10.0 each (the Australians were paid £30 per Test), and where public anger, which had been steadily mounting, came close to bursting through the pickets and the England dressing-room door. Mounted troopers stood by. The crowd had become inflamed by the horrible blow inflicted over Australian captain Bill Woodfull's heart by a ball from Larwood —and the sequel. When Woodfull was well enough to resume, Jardine switched his field from orthodox to Bodyline. It seemed to many to be an instance of kicking a man when he was down. When later in the innings Oldfield's skull was fractured when he mishooked Larwood the fury was widespread. During the match, Warner visited the Australian dressing-room and was told by Woodfull that only one of the teams was playing cricket. The Australian Board of Control, having prepared a cable of protest to MCC at Lord's, fired it off. It read:

Bodyline bowling assumed such proportions as to menace best interests of game, making protection of body by batsmen the main consideration, and causing intensely bitter feeling between players, as well as injury. In our opinion it is unsportsmanlike, and unless stopped at once is likely to upset friendly relations existing between Australia and England.

The bitter feeling was probably best expressed by Vic Richardson (grandfather of Ian and Greg Chappell), who scored a valiant 83 as opening batsman in the fourth Test, at Brisbane, and was big enough to fraternise with the Englishmen when fraternisation no longer seemed natural. He was not, however, fraternising when he responded to Larwood's apology for almost hitting him with a short one: 'If it happens again I'll knock your bloody block off!'

MCC took a few days to reply to the Australian Board's cable, and an uncompromising reply it was:

We, the Marylebone Cricket Club, deplore your cable message and deprecate the opinion that there has been unsports-

manlike play. We have the fullest confidence in our captain, team, and managers, and are convinced that they would do nothing to infringe the Laws of cricket or the spirit of the game. We have no evidence that our confidence is misplaced. Much as we regret the accidents to Woodfull and Oldfield, we understand that in neither case was the bowler to blame. If the Board wishes to propose a new Law or rule it shall receive our careful consideration in due course. We hope that the situation is not now as serious as your cable appears to indicate, but if it is such as to jeopardise the good relations between English and Australian cricketers, and you consider it desirable to cancel the remainder of the programme, we would consent with great reluctance.

Cable No. 2 from Australia reaffirmed that England's peculiar hostility was 'opposed to the spirit of cricket' and 'dangerous to players', assured MCC that cancellation was not considered necessary, and promised a report in due course, when the specially-appointed committee consisting of Roger Hartigan, M. A. Noble, Woodfull and Richardson had completed its deliberations. Dr E. P. Barbour, writing in the *Sydney Mail*, likened it to a backyard squabble between two schoolboys: 'Mrs Smith called Mrs Brown on the telephone and said, "My little boy says your boy is throwing stones at him"; and Mrs Brown replied, very haughtily, "I am sure my little boy would not dream of throwing stones; and if you don't like it you can tell him to take his toys and come home."'

Honour was satisfied for both sets of administrators, but play continued, tensely, uncomfortably, and sometimes painfully. England were to win four of the five Tests, only the second, at Melbourne, going against them. It was there, after missing the opening Test, that Bradman made his only century of the series. It followed an inglorious duck in the first innings, when he dragged a long hop from Bowes into his wicket first ball. His return to the pavilion was one of the longest and most silent of his distinguished career.

The inventive Bradman found his own method of dealing

with Bodyline, skipping to leg and hitting to the almost unguarded off side, but his contribution of only 396 runs in eight innings at 56.57, though placing him top of the Australian averages and representing a performance of which any other batsman would have been distinctly proud, spelt failure by his gigantic standards. Larwood, the arch executioner, took his wicket four times out of seven, and finished with 33 wickets at 19.51. Sixteen of his victims were clean bowled, many of them positioned towards leg in anticipation of the 'rib ball' which followed them. From such a remote stance there was no way of countering the lethal yorker.

It could be said of this torrid series that, like Gallipoli and Tobruk, it offered opportunities for heroism unparalleled in normal combat. The bombardment endured by Woodfull, Fingleton, Richardson, Darling, Ponsford and O'Brien, in one Test by the stylish Kippax, and throughout the series by the even more defenceless batsmen of the lower order evoked the sympathy of the entire nation (apart from a few who felt that the old-timers could have dealt with it!), and from many overseas observers. Bradman, of the twinkling feet and keen eye, avoided injury if not occasional perplexity, but the one truly outstanding innings of the series came, in the first Test, at Sydney, from Stanley Joseph McCabe, chunky, 22-year-old, prematurely bald, country-born batsman from New South Wales, who plundered 187 runs, unbeaten, off the England attack, hooking, pulling, slashing, parrying, with the little luck that even a Ranjitsinhji would have needed.

His grandmother had withstood bushrangers; with open, round countenance squarely facing Larwood and Voce, McCabe beat away England's attack with his flailing bat. 'If I happen to get hit out there, Dad,' he said before resuming his innings, 'keep Mum from jumping the fence and laying into these Pommy bowlers!'

He did all the 'laying in' himself, sending the Sydney onlookers into an hysteria of excitement. When the innings ended for 360 on the second day McCabe had been batting for four hours and had hit 25 fours. He had been dropped only twice, at 159 in the gully off Voce and at 170 at slip off Larwood. It was the innings of a lifetime (except that he played two equally swashbuckling, but in different circumstances, in South Africa in 1935–36 and England in 1938) but it was not to be repeated in the 1932–33 series. On reflection, it may not have done Australia's cause a lot of good, since those with hard hearts were able to point to it as an example of what could be done against the short-pitched ball, viewing it as batting at its most dramatic and therefore most enthralling.

The English camp was shocked by Jeff Thomson's hostility in 1974–75 in spite of some hotly-worded advance publicity. So it could be said of Australia in 1932–33: the selection of the MCC side must have offered a few clues of what lay ahead, particularly for those who had read of one or two stormy incidents during the preceding English season. Arthur Carr, the Notts captain, had encouraged Larwood and Voce to bowl Bodyline in several county matches, though Larwood's famed accuracy seemed to fail him, and without it the leg-side attack looked quite scrappy. (Carr himself once fell flat on his posterior in dodging a bouncer from Surrey's Maurice Allom, saying gravely as he picked himself up, 'This is no way to play cricket!'.) And there was the notorious occasion at The Oval when Bill Bowes dropped a few short at Jack Hobbs, who was then in his fiftieth year, though making runs galore. Hobbs ostentatiously walked way down the pitch and patted the spot where the bouncer had pitched, there was some banter, and that might have been the end of the matter, except that one newspaper report ran:

Bowes must alter his tactics. Bowes bowled with five men on the on side, and sent down several very short-pitched balls which repeatedly bounced head high and more. Now that is not bowling; indeed, it is not cricket, and if all the fast bowlers were to adopt his methods, MCC would be compelled to step in and penalise the bowler who bowled

*the ball less than halfway up the pitch.... I appeal to
Bowes, and to others, if any, who may have influenced him
to his present style to get him back to orthodoxy.... Later
Macaulay sent down two fast full-pitches to the Surrey
captain. Very coolly Mr Jardine ducked and the first 'header'
went for four byes.*

The writer was none other than P. F. 'Plum' Warner, soon to
be in the ineffectual position, despite his overall power in
the game, of manager of the MCC side captained by the
aforementioned Mr Jardine, whose coolness was never in
dispute.

Jardine, through Percy Fender, invited Carr and his two
fast bowlers, Larwood and Voce, to dinner at the Piccadilly
Hotel some time before the tour and the four discussed 'leg
theory'. Jardine developed his strategy further by study-
ing scoring charts of the main Australian batsmen compiled
by the popular little scorer-baggageman Bill Ferguson, and
by frequently visiting Frank Foster at his St James's flat to
discuss the left-hander's field placings on the 1911–12 tour
of Australia. Foster later asked his friends in Australia to
forgive him for innocently contributing to the English
tactics in 1932–33. 'I am sorry my experience and advice
were put to such an unworthy use,' he wrote.

With or without Foster's assistance, Jardine's plan would
have been carried out. During the preliminary match against
South Australia, Vic Richardson asked Voce what sort of
side had been brought out. The reply froze him in his
tracks: 'If we don't beat you, we'll knock your bloody
heads off.'

Harold Larwood, born at Nuncargate, a Nottinghamshire mining village, on November 14, 1904 (the same day as
Michael Ramsey, Archbishop of Canterbury!), left school
at thirteen and was a pony-boy in the pits at fourteen. At
seventeen he was captivated by the sight of Fred Barratt
(who had once broken *two* stumps in bowling R. H.
Williams of Worcestershire) dismissing the mighty Jack
Hobbs. At eighteen he was having a trial at Trent Bridge, all

5 ft 4 ins of him, pale and frail and fast. He was signed on at thirty-two shillings a week, and was coached by Fred Barratt, who taught him to swing the ball, and Jim Iremonger, who trained him to run in smoothly, retain balance, and follow through. He practised hard and did his ground duties, one of which was cleaning pads and boots. One day he lovingly whitened Maurice Tate's boots and received for his trouble a two-shilling piece. Two years later he was opening England's bowling with the great man of Sussex.

Soon after he entered the Notts XI, filling out to twelve stone and attaining 5 ft 9 ins, word spread that here was an express bowler out of the ordinary. The coaches had done their job well. The run-up was smooth and silent, the leap composed and balanced, long left arm high, the plunge of the front foot giving maximum pull. His below-average height was an assistance if anything, the short-of-a-length ball coming at the chin rather than over the head. Arthur Carr recalled how 'Lol' Larwood enjoyed bowling batsmen out : 'Whenever he hit the stumps a broad smile came across his face which he tried to conceal. It would not interest him if somebody was *caught* off his bowling.'

After a quiet maiden Test match, his second appearance for England was distinguished, not only for his three wickets in each innings but for his side's victory at The Oval in 1926 to regain the Ashes. Several England slips fieldsmen left Kennington with ugly bruises on their hands.

Stories of Larwood's speed and hostility were legion, and bred. More than one batsman is alleged to have headed for the pavilion after playing and missing. 'You're all right. You didn't touch it. You're not out !' would say the wicketkeeper. 'Maybe,' would say the proverbial batsman, 'but I'm going !' Against an Indian touring team he and Voce bet a packet of smokes as to who would hit a particular batsman's turban first. Film exists of the wretched Sikh's assisted exit from the field, forehead garnished with a bump the size of a pigeon's egg. After lunch was often the worst time to be facing the Notts fast men, when they had had a few refreshing pints. Or when captain or umpire had cunningly expressed the belief that the old speed wasn't there. Frank Chester (who, incidentally, considered his old Worcestershire colleague Burns fastest of all) mischievously compared Larwood's speed unfavourably with Learie Constantine's during the 1928 series, and within a few overs 'Lol' had struck Martin on the head, spun his cap-peak sideways, and turned Challenor's cap back to front. 'This was Larwood at his fastest; it seemed to be that the moment the ball left his hand it was at the opposite end of the pitch.' The Hampshire players were never to forget one afternoon when a telegram was brought onto the field for Larwood. He read it, put it in his pocket, and proceeded to bowl at a speed none of them thought possible. At the end of that blistering session it was the least the Hampshiremen could do to enquire of the theme of the message. It had been to the effect that Mrs Larwood had given birth to a daughter (she was to present her husband with five in all). 'Thank God it wasn't twins!' murmured one of the aggrieved batsmen.

He toured Australia with Chapman's highly successful 1928–29 side, though after a few overs, when the shine had been grazed off the ball, he proved to be only mildly penetrative. In the 1930 Tests, in three of which he played, he managed only four wickets for 292. By 1932, then, he was no certainty to tour Australia again. By taking 162 wickets at 12·86 and heading the national averages, and by maintaining a renown for speed and—more importantly—accuracy, which Jardine counted essential to his plan, Larwood ensured his place in the side. He knew what was expected of him, especially after the dinner with Jardine at the Piccadilly, and as a professional cricketer he prepared himself. He inflicted pain, he created embarrassment, he was abused by the masses, he was spat upon and he received vile letters. He was cheered to the echo when he scored 98 in the fifth Test, at Sydney. At times he had to have police protection. The heat drained him, and the pounding over hard grounds tortured his feet and wrecked his boots. But he was there at the end, a hero to many, especially among those closest to him.

The aftermath of the Bodyline series was soaked in hypocrisy and piety. Larwood was asked by MCC to apologise for his tactics, something he could see no justification in doing. He had played the last of his 21 Tests. In 1936 he headed the English averages but was unavailable for Australia. Had he gone it is doubtful whether he could have withstood the physical strain as his foot, damaged in Australia, gave him recurring discomfort even after an operation in 1933 for a fractured sesamoid bone.

After having resisted tempting offers to tell his story to the newspapers immediately upon arrival home, he finally opened his heart to the *Sunday Express*, and his unrepentant words and condemnation of Australian spectators, the Australian Board, and Australian batsmanship fanned the flames. Where would it end? That same month MCC called a meeting at Lord's to enquire into the events of the tour, Australia already having framed a new rule against intimidatory bowling. The shutters were being unlocked and would soon be rattling down, hiding from view an unsavoury confusion without silencing the echoes.

Before the new Law was passed for universal acceptance in November, 1934, there were instances of direct attack by fast bowlers. In 1933 in the Test match against West Indies at Old Trafford, Jardine himself withstood a withering assault to put together his one century for England. Earlier in the innings Hammond had suffered a split chin, returning after stitches to have a few friendly words with bowler Constantine, who refrained from bouncing any more at him. Jardine was hit all over but never flinched. Some saw him as paying penance, but it is highly unlikely that he viewed it that way. It was also rumoured that certain authorities had requested that this display of Bodyline be performed for the benefit of those who had not seen it in Australia and wished to assess it first-hand.

In 1934, with Jardine retired and Larwood and Voce *persona non grata*, it was E. W. 'Nobby' Clark, Northamptonshire's fair-haired, highly-strung, and often brilliant left-arm fast bowler, who gave the Australians some thoughtful moments as he smacked the ball down with a ring of leg-side fieldsmen. But the worst was past, and the Law, written in, killed speculation about whether Bodyline was decent or not.

Jardine's name lives on, deeply respected by some who knew him well, despised by Australians in general. They were irritated by his multi-coloured Harlequin cap and un-smiling visage. 'Leave our flies alone!' he had been warned loudly as he swatted them away from his sweating brow ... with the cutting addendum, 'They're the only friends you've got anyway!' It has been suggested that a gesture—just the slightest acknowledgement, with humour—might have eased the atmosphere during those hot rumbustious afternoons. But the effect could not have been altered materially.

Harold Larwood, who at his peak was timed at 96 mph (how reliably is difficult to judge), was a victim of the aftermath. Jardine withdrew from the game without ever uttering the faintest regret. Arthur Carr was sacked from the Notts captaincy in 1934 for standing by Bill Voce, who continued to bowl leg theory on occasions (including Notts' match against the 1934 Australians, when he took 8 for 66 in the first innings and was 'injured' in the second after complaints from the touring side) and remained a Test player, touring Australia in 1936–37 and ten years later. A kind of Bodyline was bowled here and there, but never as flagrantly during the infamous tour and never with the speed and relentless accuracy of Larwood.

Larwood's later years were to produce the most extraordinary of ironies. In 1950 he emigrated with his wife and family to Australia, the land where he had been reviled, and from the instant of his landing he was gladly received. It was not until 1968 that he revisited England, briefly, and he could speak only of his sense of belonging in Australia. It was years before he regained his appetite for the game, but happily it became a custom for visiting

English cricketers to call upon him, and one of the highlights for young fast bowlers Chris Old and Mike Hendrick during the 1974–75 tour of Australia was their meeting with the kindly, grey-haired 70-year-old who had once been the idol of his country yet the target of hatred.

He expounded his creed in his autobiography:

Purely defensive batting reduces the speed bowler to panting futility. That is why he must drop a few short. In doing so, he puts the dynamite into cricket. Every fast bowler in history has done that. And when he does drop one short everybody knows it is a ball intended to intimidate, to unsettle, to test the batsman's combination of skill and nerve. When the fast bowler is no longer permitted to make the ball rear at the batsman, cricket can no longer be regarded as a manly game.... I never bowled to injure a man in my life. Frighten them, intimidate them, yes. I had a very unspectacular record of causing serious injuries to batsmen.

He then refers to Oldfield's head injury; South African H. B. 'Jock' Cameron's, sustained while trying to hook at Lord's in 1929 and which really worried Larwood; Reg Sinfield of Gloucestershire, who was laid out for an hour after being hit on the head in a county match in 1934; and Patsy Hendren, a magnificent hooker who paid the price in 1931 when he mistimed a bouncer from Larwood at Lord's. The chilling background to this last accident was that Larwood had jokingly told Mrs Hendren that morning that he was going to 'knock his block off'. The bowler was greatly relieved to find his victim sitting up in bed when he visited hospital that evening, for he had last seen him with his legs twitching as he was carried off unconscious. Hendren was playing again three weeks later, having devised a cap with three peaks (though apparently he never wore it).

It will, of course, never be known what effect on the 1932–33 Test series retaliation by Australia would have had, assuming there had been a bowler of Larwood's capabilities available. Almost certainly Woodfull would not have permitted it. 'Bull' Alexander bounced a few during his one appearance, but apart from the 6 ft 6 ins Nagel, who took 8 for 32 against MCC for a Combined XI (with an elastic bandage around his elbow after an encounter with a crank handle) and who played in the first Test, Tim Wall incredibly carried the Australian fast bowling on his own. Cricket's intelligentsia was quick to detect the attempts among boy cricketers in the parks to emulate the headline-makers, and fears grew that the game as it had been cherished for two centuries would give way to a form of violence beyond comprehension, with ghastly casualty lists for as long as the game took to perish. Retaliation would probably have hastened a general debasement at other levels. Woodfull's manly restraint and the dearth of genuine Australian pace were a mercy, though memories proved long when later generations brought forth express bowlers who were encouraged in club bars and behind dressing-room doors to settle a few old scores.

There was one well-remembered act of vengeance during the tour. Eddie Gilbert, bowling for Queensland, was lustily urged to give the Englishmen a taste of their own medicine, and one ball from him did get up to cut into Jardine's hip. Those who expected him to hold the injury or show pain did not know their Jardine. He collapsed when he reached the sanctity of the dressing-room and as fellow players slipped his trousers away they found blood on his shirt-tail.

Bill Voce was, apart from Bill Bowes, the one central character of the whole explosive saga to survive, somehow, the traumatic after-events. Burly, swarthy, he had begun as a slow bowler, but soon made his name as a distinctly awkward fast left-arm bowler whose pounding run to the wicket was filled with menace. Five years younger than Larwood, his county colleague, that is to say, only 23 when he first went to Australia in 1932–33, he eventually left behind him the unusual record of having toured Australia three times and played for England in eleven Tests against the oldest enemy *all in Australia*. He played a further sixteen Tests home and away against other countries and took 98 wickets for England in all at 27·88. By comparison, Larwood took 78 wickets in 21 Tests at 28·41.

Voce, known as 'Tangy', could make the ball move away as well as leap at a batsman's throat from outside off stump. It was his sweet satisfaction to return to Australia in 1936–37 and take 17 wickets for 133 in the first two Tests, won by England. Australia pulled the series out of the fire by winning the remaining three, Voce having strained his back, and, after a world war, when he went with Hammond's 1946–47 side he was 37, bulkier and unable to produce the fire of old. But he had his memories, and gave also to his thousands of admirers the memory of a magnificent action in which all the power of a huge body was harnessed into an awesome final delivery stride. Menacing around the wicket bringing the ball into the batsman or over the wicket running it away, it was in the latter style that he bemused the Australians during the '36–37 series. By then he was also making a few runs, and in a non-Championship match he actually reached a century in three quarters of an hour.

A fast bowler who had no pretensions to batting was W. E. 'Bill' Bowes. But he was an extremely skilful fast bowler, well over six feet tall, and able to swerve the ball from leg to off. A Yorkshireman through and through, he first played regularly in 1931, though under contract to MCC at Lord's. His run to the wicket was ungainly, almost shambling, the effect heightened by the high professorial forehead and spectacles. In the field he was not the most agile of mid-offs, but his purpose, when he had the ball— new or worn—between his fingers, was plain : to confuse and sometimes intimidate the batsman. His advance to the stumps culminated in a right-foot-behind-left shuffle, and the wrist played a noticeable part in the mechanics of this thoughtful bowler. His autobiography, *Express Deliveries*, is one of the more interesting of books written by cricketers and after retirement, his internment in Italy during the war having cost him four stone in weight, he wrote, perceptively, for 26 years for a Yorkshire newspaper, finishing in 1973 with the tied match against Middlesex at Bradford.

Bowes played fifteen times for England, against five countries, once after the war, against India, in Alec Bedser's first Test. He took part in only one of the Bodyline Tests, and took only one wicket. But it was Bradman's. In 1934 he got through an enormous amount of work in three Tests against the high-scoring Australians, and four years later, at The Oval during Hutton's match (England 903 for 7 declared; Hutton 364), Bowes took 5 for 49 and 2 for 25 against the dispirited visitors. Like many of his breed, he was charming company off the field and had a ready sense of humour (he was an adept card conjurer); but nature provided him with fast bowlers' equipment and he could use it uncompromisingly.

The same could be said of Ken Farnes, of Cambridge University, Essex and England, who also played in fifteen Test matches, with conspicuous success in several. Yet some of his most memorable displays came for the Gentlemen against the Players—first in 1936, when he spectacularly knocked Gimblett's, Hammond's and Hardstaff's stumps out of the ground, then in 1938, when he was disposed to show the national selectors how wrong they had been to omit him from the England XI. In one of the fastest overs ever bowled at Lord's, the first ball roared off a lifeless pitch; the second, in line with the batsman, did the same, flattening Bill Edrich, who was caught via glove and forehead; Price, the nightwatchman, survived one more fireball before touching another to Hammond, who caught the red blur at slip; then Eddie Paynter managed to skip out of the way of the final two balls of the evening. Wally Hammond as well as the batsmen considered it the fastest over they had seen, and Farnes was just as determined the following day, finishing with 8 for 43. Frank Woolley then 51 years old, scored 41 in further proof of his legendary class.

Farnes took ten wickets in his first Test, which was against Australia at Trent Bridge in 1934, but quite as heroic was his 6 for 96 in an Australian innings of 604 at Melbourne in the decisive fifth Test of the 1936–37 series. Most of the English players needed ice packs during the intervals.

Well over six feet tall, quite heavily built and darkly handsome, Kenneth Farnes became a master at Worksop College. His chief weapon had always been the lift he obtained from his great height. His run was not long, but his action was impressive. In the University match of 1932 he was beset by the problem of over-stepping, being no-balled 21 times, but it was not to be a recurring blemish. Most of the problems were to be the batsmen's, as they tried to score from good-length balls that perversely jumped brainward.

At Lord's in the Test against Australia in 1938 he narrowly missed a hat-trick, bowling O'Reilly, having McCormick caught by Barnett, then having Fleetwood-Smith dropped by Compton at slip. Whatever his feelings at the time, he was later able to look upon the near-miss calmly and rationally enough to write that this may have saved the match for England, since Brown (who carried his bat for 206) and his number eleven batted over half an hour on a pitch affected by rain and upon which McCormick, Australia's speed merchant, would have been distinctly menacing.

That winter he toured South Africa and finished second to left-arm spinner Hedley Verity in the Test averages, with sixteen wickets at 32.43. Only one match was decided, the third, at Durban, and Farnes's 4 for 29 and 3 for 80 against a strong Springbok batting line-up was his last winning effort for England on the cricket field. At the outbreak of war he joined the Royal Air Force, trained in Canada, and was killed when the aircraft he was flying crashed one October night in 1941. He was 30, and in his brief hurricane of a career he had taken 720 wickets at just over 20 apiece. His loss and that of Verity were to weaken England's stocks in the difficult immediate post-war seasons.

Another whose career was shortened by Hitler's war was Alf Gover, who bowled fast and furiously for Surrey for a dozen seasons or more after a brief acquaintance with

Essex. His 'knees-and-elbows' approach to the wicket was often described as resembling a man running after a bus whose speed was just slightly in excess of his own. Nevertheless, the final action was near copybook, well put together, with a fluent followthrough. Gover cheerfully faced up, season after season, to the depressing prospect of playing half his matches on the doped Oval wickets. To this was added the extra handicap of being unlucky with catches. He suffered more than the average with spilt slips chances, a further test of his temperament and wry humour.

In 1935 he took four wickets in four balls at Worcester, and in 1936 he dismissed 200 batsmen at an average of 17·73 —the first time since 1898 (Tom Richardson) that a Surrey fast bowler had taken 200 wickets. He did it again the following year, and was chosen twice against New Zealand, having had a wicketless Test debut the previous season against India. That marked the end of his international honours, apart from a Test appearance against India in 1946. He was vying with such men as Bowes, Farnes, Allen, Voce, Wellard, 'Hopper' Read, Wyatt, Jim Smith, Copson, Nichols, Perks, and Austin Matthews, all of whom—as well as Edrich and Hammond—opened the bowling for England in the period 1935 to 1939.

One of the favourite Alf Gover anecdotes concerned an early meeting with Patsy Hendren. Gover was young and Hendren was old, and he told the new fast bowler that his eyesight wasn't what it used to be and that he'd appreciate it if he didn't bounce any at him. Gover did—of course. It was something any professional fast bowler worth his salt would have done. But Hendren, an inveterate and wonderful hooker, pasted him everywhere, and it took a senior team-mate to point out the deception to Gover. The same Alfred Gover once began a match in India with his usual longish run-up, delivery of the ball, and headlong continuation past gully and off into the pavilion. It was something in the curry!

His playing days behind him, Gover turned to writing for newspapers and to expanding his cricket school in Wandsworth, where many a fast bowler (and batsman) sorted out technical hitches or developed under his tuition. The most recent was Andy Roberts, who, with batsman Vivian Richards, was sent for a coaching course by the Antigua cricket community in 1973. Hardly more than a year later Roberts was playing for West Indies, and by 1975 he was considered by many to be the fastest bowler in the world.

The two outstanding Australian fast bowlers of the 1930s were Tim Wall and Ernie McCormick, yet neither was continuously fit or penetrative enough to have been able to append his name to an era. Wall, a South Australian, whose opening partner in several Tests was the medium-pacer Alan Fairfax, troubled England quite often, starting in his first Test, which was the last one of the 1928–29 series, the only one won by Australia and which marked the beginning of a new and successful side. In that match at Melbourne he took 3 for 123 and 5 for 66, getting the mighty Hammond in each innings. As Hammond's record for the series at the start of that match was 851 runs (two single- and two double-centuries) at an average of 141·80, Australia's relief may be easily understood.

Wall's rawness was exposed on the 1930 tour of England. He had a long, flowing approach and a vigorous kicking action, but his length and direction were often at fault. He had stamina, which is always useful but never sufficient in itself, and he could move the ball. Most of all he had the ability to lift a ball nastily around a batsman's head. In four Tests in 1932–33 he took sixteen wickets at only 25·56 each, topping the Australian averages. But his speed could not be compared with that of Larwood, and Australians could not regard him as being in the Gregory-McDonald class. That season he devastated New South Wales at Sydney with all ten wickets in an innings for 36—nine of them after lunch for five runs, including four in an over. It was 33 years before this feat was emulated: by Peter Allan, the Queensland opening bowler (10 for 61 at Melbourne).

McCormick, from Victoria, began his Test career during the 1935–36 Australian tour of South Africa, and shook

England once or twice during the series in Australia a year later, removing Stan Worthington with the first ball of the series. When he had taken 3 for 26 off eight overs he had to retire with his repeated curse, lumbago, which was also to dog him on the 1938 tour of England. Then, when he showed his ability especially at Lord's, he lent his name to cricket's endless list of 'might-have-beens' when he was forced to miss the final Test at The Oval. Len Hutton made his world Test record score of 364 and England declared at an all-time high of 903 for 7—yet Australians will always claim that this could never have happened if McCormick, who had troubled Hutton earlier in the season, had been playing. Australia's opening attack was in the very limited hands of Mervyn Waite and Stan McCabe.

McCormick, who measured out a run of 31 paces, has a comical record to his name—that of being no-balled 35 times during his first match in England, at Worcester in 1938. He had real pace, venomous pace, and he brought the ball awkwardly into the batsman. But he was never master of the away-swinger. That, and his fitness problems, debarred him from joining the greats. There have been countless others in that category, high on the list being R. J. A. 'Jack' Massie, who some years earlier had earned lofty praise from Australian cricketer and journalist Johnny Moyes: 'In skill, intelligence, and downright hostility he was the finest Australian left-hand bowler I have ever seen.' Six feet four, Massie was a champion cricketer, footballer, oarsman and athlete, and his long loping run ended with a menacing sweep of the arm and a fast, curving, dipping ball which, if pitched right, was virtually unplayable. At the outbreak of the Kaiser's war he had a glittering career before him. By 1918 he was a cripple, shot through the foot in France.

Of the pre-war South Africans, Bob Crisp was one of the most outstanding. Not quite as fast as George Bisset before him, Crisp had the pace and aggression to take seven or eight (and once nine) wickets in an innings with unusual frequency in domestic matches. He is the only man to have taken four wickets with consecutive balls *twice* in first-class cricket, and he played in nine Tests against England and Australia. Another all-round athlete, born in Calcutta, Crisp could have written a fascinating autobiography—probably running to two volumes. He twice climbed Kilimanjaro in a fortnight, swam in Loch Lomond naked, ran a duck farm, wrote for newspapers in South Africa and Britain, won a DSO and MC as a commander in the Tank Corps in the desert, and eventually walked out on 'civilisation' to live on a Greek island. At Trent Bridge in 1935 he limped off with a foot inflamed by a blood blister, returned to the field, defying doctor's orders, and broke up the Leyland-Wyatt partnership by dismissing both batsmen.

South Africa possessed no bowler of excessive pace between Kotze and the battery of the 1960s, but Neville Quinn, a left-arm bowler, came off the pitch very hastily, and ranked second among medium-pacers in Don Bradman's carefully-kept book (after Tate). A. B. C. 'Chud' Langton, 6 ft 3 ins, was another to have spasmodic success. He took six wickets in South Africa's first-ever Test victory in England in 1935, and played fifteen times in Test matches before the war, which cost him his life at the age of 30. Arthur Ochse could be hostile, and headed South Africa's bowling figures against England in 1929, though he took only ten wickets. Musclebound and thick-set, Ochse came from the country, and was shocked at his first sight of London. Louis Duffus, doyen of South Africa's cricket-writers, recalled Ochse's exclamation outside Waterloo Station: 'There are more people in this street than in the whole of Graaf Reinet!' He ruined the flavour of the Springboks' match against Sir Julien Cahn's XI near Nottingham by fizzing one through Sir Julien's unprofessional defence when that grand patron had made but two runs and was 'entitled' to quite a few more.

A. J. 'Sandy' Bell, at 6 ft 4 ins, an inch taller than Bob Crisp, was not as fast, but bowled a prodigious inswinger with a hand-over-the-head action. His finest series was in Australia in 1931–32, when he took 23 wickets in five Tests, carrying the brunt of the work in a summer of slavery (Australia won all five matches by big margins). Bell's career ended when fluid developed in his elbow.

The most outstanding New Zealand fast bowler of those times was Jack Cowie, an Aucklander, a boy leg-spinner who on impulse began to bowl fast and found he had something special—a reversal of the usual pattern. His first Test wicket was Wally Hammond, and on the 1937 tour of England he took 114 wickets at just under twenty with outswingers and offcutters, gaining sharp lift. He was big—nicknamed The Bull—and *Wisden* thought of him that had he been Australian 'he might have been termed a wonder of the age'. After the war he was effective but understandably less fiery. He was 37 when he toured England with Walter Hadlee's talented 1949 team. Like so many other fast bowlers, the precious years of peak fitness and sharpest speed had been taken in the putrid flood of world war.

12. ANOTHER WAR, ANOTHER IMBALANCE

Ray Lindwall—Keith Miller—irregular selections
Bob Massie—Alec Bedser—Trevor Bailey

Imitating Ray Lindwall gave exquisite pleasure, like arrowing through surf or ice-skating. There was the balanced, rhythmic run, a build-up. The eventual separation of the hands, with the left slicing a slipstream around the midriff and the right swinging to and fro, ball at fingertips. The crease approached. The right arm became a V. The left shoulder turned to the batsman (or kerosene tin). A calculated leap and the propelling arm made its circle. The tennis ball winged away and veered to the left after the roundarm slinging motion and off-cut action. It mattered hardly at all that no wicket was taken or that the ball may even have been driven for four runs into Mrs Shepherd's flowerbed. The ecstacy was in the act itself. In 1950 there were thousands of boys in Sydney practising this fantasy.

Lindwall, with Keith Miller, formed the destructive Australian force straight after the Second World War which made Bradman's and subsequently Hassett's side invincible for series after series, until England, through tears of joy and relief, regained the Ashes at The Oval in 1953. This did not mark the end of the power and influence of these fast bowlers, for Lindwall was to extend his Test career to thirteen years when he played his last Test during the tour of India and Pakistan in 1959–60. By then he was 38, and his low arm was lower still; but he had long been a complete master of his art. During his peak years he had fearsome speed—which he reserved for shock effect—a savage bouncer, the inducker, outswinger, slower ball, and cutters. He could also bat well enough to make a Test century against England and another against West Indies.

When he was a lad, Lindwall saw Larwood bowl, and endeavoured to copy him. He lived a street or two from Bill O'Reilly, Australia's great medium-pace spinner, and this was an added stimulus. He was 25 and a war veteran with lingering malaria by the time the first post-war England v Australia Test series got under way in 1946–47, and his new-ball partnership with Miller, formed in the first Test—at Brisbane, won by Australia by an innings and 332 runs—was not 'registered' until later in the series, for Lindwall went down with chickenpox. In the final match of the series he took 7 for 63 in England's first innings, and the Old Country awaited him with interest in 1948.

About 5 ft 10½ ins, fair-haired, strongly-built, Lindwall mowed his way across England, taking 86 wickets at 15·68, 27 of them in the Test matches, and his name became one with which fathers could terrorise their sons. County batsmen lost their stumps to him, Test batsmen lost their poise. Some finished in hospital, notably Jack Robertson of Middlesex, who was hit on the jaw, and Denis Compton, whose heroic 145 not out at Old Trafford was interrupted by a slit brow when he changed his leg glance into a hasty hook at the shout of 'no-ball'. Earlier, in the Trent Bridge Test, Compton had made a stirring 184 which ended when he fell on his stumps in avoiding a bumper from Miller. The Nottinghamshire members and other spectators, with memories of Larwood and Voce, were vociferous in their abuse of Australia's fast bowlers for bowling dangerously short in poor light, and it took Miller's strong fingers around his collar to quieten one critic as the players left the field.

Miller was a big, devil-may-care Victorian who had moved to New South Wales. He was a wartime pilot in Britain capable of crashlanding at 11 am and joining in a game of cricket at noon. He made his name with the Australian Services side at the end of the war, just as Gregory had done

25 years earlier, and for years he stood unchallenged as the world's premier all-rounder. Batting or fast bowling, he could appear a world-beater at either, yet a recurring back injury hampered him and sapped his appetite for bowling. As a batsman he was in his element when things were difficult. Then he would hit his way out of trouble. Defensively he was sometimes found lacking. As a slip fieldsman he brought off some of the most spectacular catches of the age, though often giving the appearance of standing bored. Similarly he needed to be in the mood for bowling, and at times he seemed to be taking it all none too seriously. He could bowl an unplayable thunderbolt off a few paces, and many were the bewildered batsmen who had served up to them bouncing googlies off five yards. His quickest, swerving, lifting delivery was feared by many batsmen even more than Lindwall's classical probing. Together they made one of cricket's most terrifying duets, abetted in 1948 by the foolish regulation whereby a new ball could be taken after 55 six-ball overs. With the clever left-arm medium-pacer Bill Johnston forming the third prong of the attack, Australia's Neptune sank many hundreds of ships with his trident.

Denis Compton, though he never took the precaution of wearing a thigh pad, unashamedly confessed that often before facing Lindwall and Miller he was a frequent visitor to the little room off the dressing-room. He was most wary of Miller—who became a close personal friend—on days following the bowler's late nights (which were the norm) when he had a hangover and felt 'mean'. Len Hutton, who with Cyril Washbrook opened many an England innings against the full, fresh shock blast of the Australian attack, dreaded the sight of the seam holding its vertical position as the ball sped towards him : after pitching it could move either way—with spiteful lift. 'Whatever defence I had,' Hutton once wrote, 'it was useless at these moments.' England's slight and pale-faced opener, whose highly distinguished Test career extended from 1937 to 1955, and whose greatest dread was of falling to the first ball of a Test match, bowled in the hush by Lindwall, was dropped for one match in 1948 after several failures. He spent most of those stormy years hoping against hope that England would one day soon have at least one bowler of real pace with whom to answer back. His prayers were eventually answered with the advent of Fred Trueman, followed by others. Hutton had been cracked on the head and sent to hospital by E. Q. Davies in MCC's match against Transvaal during the 1938–39 tour (the ball dropping on to the stumps), and during the war he broke his left arm, which was left over an inch shorter than his right after bone grafts. This was the architect of almost every England innings during the Australian post-war reign of terror.

When bumpers were for the umpteenth time the topic of general discussion in 1975, Miller, now a newspaper correspondent, wrote that they should and could never be banned. Though he never enjoyed them himself as a batsman, it was a predictable view, supported by most cricketers and followers of the game. 'Pure commonsense thinking by the umpires seems the only sane way,' he wrote; to which many would have added 'and by the bowler'. He shrewdly illustrated the point with the recollection of having bowled an entire eight-ball over of bumpers to Australia's great left-hand opening batsman Arthur Morris, most of which were hooked for four. The crowd loved it ... as presumably did Morris. Norman O'Neill, a thrilling hooker, once smashed a fusillade from fast-medium Sam Loxton the same way in a Sheffield Shield match.

Miller also recalled Bradman's cool hooking of a succession of bumpers from Yorkshire's Ron Aspinall to the boundary and saying between overs, 'Nugget, I hope they don't take him off for bowling too many bumpers!'

Miller recalled also that Freddie Brown, England's 40-year-old captain in the 1950–51 series, bluffed him and Lindwall into desisting by standing with his hand on his hip, scowling down the pitch 'like some irate schoolmaster annoyed at an offending pupil'. Brown, mainly with drives, made 62 at Melbourne and 79 at Sydney before they grew impatient with moderation.

Miller took 7 for 60 and 2 for 17 in his first Test against England, knocking Washbrook's cap off in the process, and finished with 170 wickets in his 55 Tests. Lindwall became Australia's Test record-holder with 228 in his 61 appearances, exceeded since by Benaud with 248 and McKenzie with 246. Yet at one stage it seemed his career was nearing its end when in 1954–55 he was bowling with a limp and a prayer. That tough competitor Trevor Bailey actually allowed a ball from Lindwall to bowl him, giving him his 100th wicket against England. Yet Lindwall was still around four years later to haunt England, and gave Bailey food for thought by dismissing him twice without scoring in the fifth Test at Melbourne.

Bradman's 1948 Australians, thought by many to have been the strongest of all touring sides, climaxed the series by bowling England out at The Oval for 52 and 188 and winning by an innings and 149 runs. Lindwall, off 16·1 overs, took 6 for 20 in that traumatic first innings. Yet not everyone was satisfied. Bill O'Reilly, now in the Press box, was concerned at Lindwall's drag, which, photographs proved, took him some distance over the line. He also disapproved of the persistent short-pitched bowling, which he considered practically identical to England's in 1932–33 except for the field-placing which accompanied it. It was felt by many that unless England found a fast bowler or two for the return series in 1950–51, it would be a brutal series. England could not yet come up with the fast bowler of her dreams, and the aggression, fortunately, did not reach ugly proportions. But a further year later, when the star-studded West Indies side toured Australia, Walcott, Worrell and Weekes, destroyers of English bowling, were subjected to volley after volley of searing bouncers. Australia won the series four-one and the mighty three Ws were bounced to near-impotency. No Test series ends with the final ball: when West Indies had the fire-power in later years they used it—without hesitation. There are no treaties in international cricket.

Miller's ferocity was still there in 1954–55, when he was

35. England needed only 94 in the fourth innings of the Adelaide Test to win the series, yet Miller, who had told a friend that 'somebody's in for a nasty half-hour', got rid of Hutton, Bill Edrich and Cowdrey in twenty balls, and took a glorious catch at cover to send back Peter May. As he hit the ground in securing the catch he damaged his shoulder, and this reduced his effectiveness. England got home by five wickets, but such was Miller's stature that few would have said with complete conviction that the opposition could have done so while he was fit and in such an 'impossible' mood.

In 1956, when in his 37th year and with his back ailment certainly no more comfortable, Miller bowled 34 overs in England's first innings at Lord's, taking 5 for 72, and 36 in the second, taking 5 for 80. This ranked with all the feats of stamina down the years—the tireless courage of Richardson, Jones, Cotter, Geary, Tate and Bedser.

Australia were a long time replacing Lindwall and Miller as an established match-winning pair. During the 1940s and 1950s fast bowlers came and went, winning an Australian cap or two, but never showing out as natural successors. Fred Freer had played once, when Lindwall was ill in 1946; Len Johnson of Queensland played once, against India at Melbourne, and was left to reflect on his 3 for 66 and 3 for 8 (as well as 25 not out); Geoff Noblet won three Test caps, one of them during the 1949–50 tour of South Africa, when the athletic left-arm fast bowler Alan Walker came close to adding an international cricket cap to his Wallaby rugby shirt; in 1956 the tall and gangling Pat Crawford played four Tests against England and India before injury got the better of him; Ron Archer, who seemed the next Keith Miller, was also stricken with back and knee injuries and was forced into retirement after 19 Test appearances; blond trier Frank Misson played five times, Colin Guest once, Ron Gaunt three times, Des Hoare once, Gordon Rorke— one of the controversial figures of the 1958–59 series—four times before falling prey to hepatitis; Dave Renneberg played eight times in the mid-1960s; Ian Meckiff represented

Australia 18 times before his action was finally deemed illegal in 1963; Grahame Corling featured in all five Tests against England in 1964, then fell away.

Australia's new-ball attack thus rested chiefly in the capacious hands of left-hander Alan Davidson, who was supported at various times by most of those previously mentioned. Young Graham McKenzie made his debut in 1961, and Neil Hawke a year later, when Davidson was in his final season. All through the 1960s the Australian attack was unsettled. For a time it seemed that either Peter Allan, Laurie Mayne, Eric Freeman or Alan Connolly would be the ideal ally for McKenzie, particularly the last-mentioned, who played in 29 Tests and took 102 wickets. His cut, swerve and clever pace-changes beset the batsmen of several nations with insoluble problems, but two seasons with Middlesex probably sapped something of what remained. At his retirement Connolly had taken more wickets for Victoria than anyone else.

The early 1970s still found Australia without an opening pair whose names rolled off the public tongue as a dreaded cliché. A. L. 'Froggy' Thomson, who bowled with a curious wrong-foot action, was heralded as the new terror when England went to Australia in 1970, but his Test performances fell well short of his destructive displays for Victoria. Ross Duncan and Tony Dell were also tried; and in England in 1972 David Colley, one of the young hopefuls, played in three Tests. But it was another 'unknown', Bob Massie, who wrote the headlines. In his Test debut, at Lord's, he took 8 for 84 in the first innings and 8 for 53 in the second, swinging the ball about as if he had a wire attached to it. Bowling around the wicket, he mesmerised the England batsmen with the late curl of the ball, having three caught in the first innings and all eight in the second. Claims by certain reporters that Massie had rubbed sunburn cream into the ball were hotly refuted, but optimistic English suggestions that he would not be able to repeat his 'Massiecre' turned out to be justified. He took seven wickets in the remaining three Tests, and eight in two Tests at home

165

against Pakistan, and that was the end of his staggering Test career. It was said that when he lost a little of his swing and the wickets stopped tumbling at the staccato rate he tried to compensate by pushing the ball through faster; this made him easier still.

So, within months of putting together an apparent world-shattering combination of Lillee and Massie (the former took 31 wickets in the five Tests in 1972 in England), Australia had only one world-beater—enough for which to be grateful but not enough to erase the question 'When are we going to have another Lindwall and Miller?' The answer came in the 1974–75 series, when 'Lillee and Thomson' became an acceptable paraphrase. Only their endurance remained to be proved.

Seven years is not a long time in the history of man, but from 1945, when cricket began to feel its way again in exhausted and war-torn England, until 1952, when Fred Trueman first measured out his run for England, it seemed an eternity to Englishmen who longed for another Larwood to restore pride to the national Eleven. Alec Bedser had carried England's bowling on his substantial shoulders through nine Test series since the resumption—a genial giant with a striking similarity to Maurice Tate in the snappy movement of the ball off the pitch and his knack of bowling the 'dream' ball. Most of the world's top batsmen in the late 1940s and early 1950s attributed to Bedser the finest ball bowled to them. In a Test career of 51 matches he took 236 wickets, which was then unexcelled. Shingles contracted in Perth at the start of the 1954–55 tour of Australia affected his powers, but what really drew the curtains on his gallant international career was Len Hutton's belief in bowling of top speed allied with conservation of energies, i.e. a sedate over rate, meticulous field-placing between deliveries, long and leisurely walk-back to the disc marker. It was a conclusion much regretted, and echoing in many respects that of Tate twenty-two years earlier. But Bedser was to serve England as selector and tour manager, with a highly successful business behind him and his twin, Eric, enabling him to remain a powerful influence in the game for years after he had hung up his enormous boots.

Bedser's new-ball cohorts had included Bill Bowes, Bill Voce, red-haired Dick Pollard of Lancashire (5 for 24 on debut against India in 1946), Alf Gover, Bill Edrich, Jack Martin of Kent, Cliff Gladwin and George Pope, both of the long line of splendid Derbyshire fast bowlers, Harold Butler of Notts, Alec Coxon of Yorkshire, and Allan Watkins, the Glamorgan medium-pacer—all these within two years! During the 1947–48 tour of West Indies England's faster bowling was entrusted to Ken Cranston, Butler, Gubby Allen (then 45), and, to his surprise, Maurice Tremlett of Somerset.

It was not until 1949, against New Zealand, that Bedser had a fresh and promising opening bowler at the other end —the Cambridge and Essex amateur all-rounder Trevor Bailey. Though bowlers such as Les Jackson, another Derbyshire stalwart—with a powerful slinging action—and Derek Shackleton of Hampshire and John Warr of Middlesex were to make odd appearances, England's opening attack settled to Bedser and Bailey until the entry of Statham and then Trueman. Crinkly-haired Bailey's doughty batsmanship, superb slip-fielding, and general air of combativeness made him a huge asset to the side, and his performances in Australia before Lindwall broke his thumb at Sydney underlined England's gradual emergence from the shadows. His absence from the attack also brought into focus the thinness of the reserves. While Bedser rolled in for over after over and the middle-aged skipper, Freddie Brown, forsook leg-breaks for medium-pace, John Warr, another Cambridge cricketer, toiled for 73 eight-ball overs in two Tests to take one wicket for 281 runs. It was said that when Australia's Ian Johnson got a fine touch to a ball for Godfrey Evans to hold the catch, the umpire answered Warr's appeal with a gentle enquiry as to the soundness of his heart before raising his finger.

Frederick Sewards Trueman, then, was received into the hearts of English cricket-followers everywhere with great warmth and pride and gratitude. By the time his Test career came to a close he had talked and gesticulated—but most of all *bowled*—his way into the hearts of spectators the world over.

13. FRED AND GEORGE

Fred Trueman—a Test record—Brian Statham

There has been no grander sight in post-war cricket than Fred Trueman in full flight. Hefty legs swinging purposefully, commodious flannels stretched by an ample chassis, broadest of chests heaving, arms under control from beefy shoulders, wide-mouthed, pasty face shaded by a massive flop of jet-black hair. The final action was perfection. The body turned side-on, the right arm cocked back as the leading arm was hoisted, and an awesome cartwheel sent him into a followthrough which resembled a Sea Fury finishing its mission along the runway of an aircraft carrier. He swung the ball, mainly outwards, and bumped it spectacularly when he chose, and in 1952 he had India's batsmen running in all directions. He took 29 wickets in the four Tests at 13·31 each; Bedser took 20 at 13·95. At Headingley they had India nought for four wickets in the second innings, and at Old Trafford Trueman took 8 for 31, the best figures returned in Test cricket by a bowler of true pace. The batsmen were frightened, and no fast bowler, scenting this, could help but be inspired. Following on, India were out again that day for 82, Bedser and Lock now doing the damage. This was English cricket *redivivus*.

Expectation was high when Australia arrived in England in 1953. Many felt that England had the equipment with which to recover the Ashes. Yet it was not until the final Test, at The Oval, that—after four drawn matches—Trueman was chosen after passing a frustrating summer more in the National Service uniform of the Royal Air Force than in cricket gear. Australia batted, and Bedser bowled the opening over. Then Trueman, to a buzz from the crowd, was called up by Hutton to bowl from the pavilion end. Hassett took one from his first ball, then his second was a bouncer at Morris. The roar was expressive of pent-up hope. Here at last was a young Englishman who could give the Aussies a spoonful of mustard. Excitement rose again as Morris leg-glanced the last ball of the over to Compton—who dropped the catch. Trueman's first wicket was not to come until his third spell, when Neil Harvey, the dapper and high-scoring left-hander, tried to pull a bouncer and skyed the ball to Hutton, who took the catch over his shoulder as he ran in the direction of the stroke. This was the first of 307 Test wickets for Trueman in his 12-year international career. (Only West Indies spinner Lance Gibbs has exceeded this.)

He finished with 4 for 86, and bowled only two overs in the second innings, in which Laker and Lock made short work of Australia on a pitch taking spin, and England went on to win an emotional victory and thus regained the Ashes after nineteen years. Twenty-two-year-old Trueman was no longer just the toast of Yorkshire.

There were setbacks ahead. On the tour of West Indies which followed, 'Fiery Fred', as his Yorkshire captain, Norman Yardley, had wrily named him, became the victim of his own ebullience and outspokenness. As his biographer, John Arlott, wrote, he had next to no understanding of cricket politics. His relationship with his captain, Len Hutton, was anything but smooth, and the West Indian crowds were not all that enchanted with him after he broke a bone in the elderly George Headley's arm with a bouncer and hit tailender Ferguson in the face with another.

He toiled through 320 overs in eight matches on the tour, learned much—not only about cricket—and had his good conduct bonus withdrawn, without explanation. He was not asked to play for England again until after the tour of Australia in 1954–55. It was for England a time of prolific supply of fast bowlers: Statham, Loader, Jackson, Bedser, Bailey,

Ridgway, Moss, and the fastest of them all, Tyson. The selectors were in a position to be able to cold-shoulder 'problem-boy' Trueman.

He played twice against Australia in 1956, bowling heroically at Lord's, and was omitted from the 1956–57 tour of South Africa. But from then on he placed his famous form indispensably on the Test match field, taking his hundredth Test wicket in New Zealand in 1959, his two-hundredth in 1962, and his three-hundredth in 1964. He was a legend long before his final Test appearance, and easily the most popular of cricketers before the public eye. His manner became more assured, and the 'Trueman tales' accumulated fast, many of them imaginary though acceptable and fitting as if they were real. His sense of fun and mischief were intertwined, as hundreds of opposing players would testify. A friendly pre-match visit to the other dressing-room by Fred Trueman was more than a social call. It was a declaration of war, an acutely personal challenge, clothed in rollicking humour and self-caricature.

He became master of all the fast bowler's skills, and showed a new face to the Australians at Headingley in 1961, when he cut his run in the second innings and bowled cutters into worn patches, taking five wickets in 27 balls without conceding a run. His match figures were 11 for 88. Three years later on the same ground he was hammered mercilessly by Burge and Grout as he bowled a succession of bouncers at them. One thing he could never do was resist a challenge, even when—as happened very seldom—it was an ambush.

In 1963 against West Indies at Edgbaston he had his best Test match figures, 12 for 119, their attainment assisted in all probability by the presence of the dreaded West Indian fast bowlers Hall and Griffith, who were taking some of the headlines Fred felt were his by right. In 1964 he was dropped for the fourth Test against Australia, but his replacement, the large poetry-writing left-hander Fred Rumsey, had the misfortune to strike one of the best batting wickets in history, 1281 runs being scored for nineteen wickets. Trueman came back for the Oval match, and became the first man to take 300 wickets in Tests. Neil Hawke edged him to Cowdrey, and all was joy and ovation. He was not asked to tour South Africa that winter—and had some interesting things to say when, in an emergency, England had Ian Thomson and Ken Palmer opening the bowling there. In 1965 he played twice against New Zealand to finish his Test career with 307 wickets from 67 Tests at a cost of only 21·57 each.

The 14 lb 1 oz baby who had come to cricket via the coal pit and whom Bill Bowes had assisted during the vital years was not finished yet. He could still be incited by a 'fancy' cap to threaten to pin the wearer of it to 'bloody sight-screen', and though the old edge of speed was gone forever he still had an occasional hour of glory. He even led Yorkshire to an innings victory over the 1968 Australians. Then came retirement, reconsideration, rejection, and scattered appearances with Derbyshire. He developed a cabaret act, was voted pipe-smoker of the year, raised money for charities, wrote for a newspaper, did radio comment, added an honest and unobjectionable wit to the Press boxes. Always he will be remembered as almost—if not *the* (by his own conclusion)—'finest fast bowler that ever drew breath'.

Fred Trueman's partner through so many countless hours of Test match action was Brian Statham, known as 'George', 'Whippet', or 'Greyhound'. He was extraordinarily loose-limbed and resilient and seemingly tireless. Often he had the end into which the wind was blowing, and often he was taken to task by commentators and admiring fellow-players for bowling *too* accurately. He did not always seem to be enjoying even reasonable luck—beating the edge, grazing the stumps—but the unwavering accuracy and endurance paid off handsomely over the years.

Statham played in more Tests—seventy—than any other fast bowler, taking 252 wickets and winning the respect and admiration of everyone with whom he came into contact. His bouncer, which he used discreetly, was particularly nasty, but batsmen feared most of all his 'nip-backer', the ball which kissed the turf outside off stump and cut in viciously to win him hundreds of wickets for Lancashire and England. The 1935 amendment to the lbw Law was made for bowlers of his type, batsmen previously having been spared if the ball pitched outside off stump was prevented by their pads from hitting the stumps.

Statham was a magnificent outfielder with a strong arm just as Trueman was a mighty asset at short leg. They both had their moments as batsmen, Trueman hitting with enormous power in the lower order and Statham, left-handed with the bat, proving obstinate enough at Sydney in 1954 to extend the tenth wicket in each innings by 43 and 46. England won the match by 38 runs.

His best spells of bowling included 7 for 39 against South Africa at Lord's in 1955 when the tourists needed 183 to win. They made 111, McGlew, upon whom so much rested, falling scoreless to Statham for the second time in the match. The Lancastrian bowled 29 overs unchanged through the innings, Trueman chipping in (literally) when he struck South Africa's captain Cheetham on the elbow and forced him out of the match.

This was a match—and a series—out of the ordinary in that both sides had an outstanding fast attack. Here at Lord's Neil Adcock and Peter Heine paired up for the first time in a Test match. Trueman and Statham v Adcock and Heine was a heavyweight tag-match indeed.

Another of Statham's sterling achievements was at Melbourne in 1958–59, when he took seven Australian wickets for 57. England's subsequent collapse for 87 almost broke his stout heart.

Statham, of the rubbery limbs and lazy smile, was awarded the CBE in 1966, and captained Lancashire from 1965 to 1967. In his final match, which was Ken Higgs's benefit at Old Trafford, he took 6 for 34, putting Yorkshire out for 61. A happy ending to a splendid career.

Trueman and Statham—'Fred and George'—served England nobly for over a decade from the early 'fifties, yet right in the middle of this glorious era for English cricket there came and went a bowler of incredible pace who made one Test series his own. He was also Lancashire-born, just ten days before Statham, in June 1930. But the county did not want him and he went instead to Northamptonshire. His rise was, as they say, meteoric, and his decline was, somewhat predictably, almost as swift. While he was at his peak his name was synonymous with terror. This was Frank Holmes Tyson.

14. 'THE GLAD ANIMAL ACTION'

Frank Tyson—1954–55 series won by speed

'To bowl quick,' Frank Tyson wrote in his autobiography (*A Typhoon Called Tyson*), 'is to revel in the glad animal action; to thrill in physical prowess and to enjoy a certain sneaking feeling of superiority over the other mortals who play the game. No batsman likes quick bowling, and this knowledge gives one a sense of omnipotence.'

He could not recall a time when he did not want to bowl as fast as humanly possible, and by the time he had shortened his excessive run and found his rhythm for the second Test match of the 1954–55 tour of Australia few onlookers could recall a cricket ball bowled faster. The delivery was no more—or less—than a flash, a blur. The ball hardly deviated. As with Kortright, it really had no need to at that speed. Tyson and Statham were timed in Wellington in 1955 at slightly under 90 mph, but it is certain that, flat out, Tyson was appreciably faster.

He announced himself to the 1953 Australians with several snorters at the early batsmen, and word went round, as it does, that here was someone out of the ordinary. In Australia he made no impression to start with, and at Brisbane, in the first Test, when Australia ran up 601 for 8 and won by an innings, he took 1 for 160. At Sydney, however, he bowled off a reduced run, but at the same hot pace on a rather more sympathetic pitch, and took 4 for 59. When he batted, a bouncer from Lindwall, in retaliation for one from Tyson, had him turning his head, ostrich-like, to be hit squarely on the back of the skull with a smack that echoed all round the ground. Carried off with a lump visible from over a hundred yards, he later continued his innings and went on to bowl like a man possessed when Australia set about scoring 223 for victory. With 6 for 85, including Lindwall's wicket, bowled as the batsman left a lot of air between himself and the stumps, Tyson swept England to a dramatic 38-run win to level the series. With Statham's great-hearted support from the other end, he blew holes in Australia's batting line-up with yorkers and flyers, bringing out Neil Harvey's true greatness as the little left-hander parried, glanced and cut his way to an undefeated 92. Classic fast bowling parenthesizing classic batsmanship.

There was better to come. At Melbourne, on a poor pitch, after Miller had taken 3 for 5 off nine overs before lunch on the first day, Statham's 5 for 60 had prevented Australia from taking too long a lead, and when England managed 279 in their second innings Australia needed 240. They made 111, Tyson taking 7 for 27 (6 for 16 off his last 51 balls). The brilliant leg-side catch with which Godfrey Evans dismissed Harvey was the turning point.

Thus Tyson was the name on everyone's lips. This broad-shouldered, balding, scholarly-looking man had shot Australia out before lunch on a day when 60,000 people at the Melbourne Cricket Ground expected to see a long, tense struggle. The batsmen had been no match. England's discovery, with his shuffling launch, giant, raking steps, and spring-steel spine-action, had, with his laser-beam bowling, given his side a victory weapon. Both sides had batsmen, bowlers and all-rounders of established reputation, but the side with a bowler of 'Typhoon's' pace—so long as he remained fit—had to win.

And win they did, though the match at Adelaide was not over until Miller's last-day flames had been extinguished by injury. England's five-wicket victory (Tyson 6 for 132) gave them a three-one lead, and the fifth Test was barely a contest since the first three days were rained off. Even then there was something of interest when Tyson bowled: wishing to rush through the overs in an outside bid for victory, Hutton asked him to bowl off just half-a-dozen paces. He still propelled the ball with sufficient vigour to knock the bat from Miller's hands. Throughout the series live-wire wicketkeeper Evans had waited in the far distance, taking the ball airborne or leaping sideways.

Tyson inflicted physical damage all along the way. Bill Edrich spilt blood at Lord's when hit on the cheekbone, and his cousin John, just as fearless, had a knuckle smashed first by Trueman and later Tyson, and had to have the bone junction surgically rebuilt. Not surprisingly, a whole army of batsmen, winded, bruised, and nursing split fingers, could have been collected. Tyson himself was not free from disability. The strain on his ankles told, and he missed Test matches at the stage when he might have been expected to continue with his Australian carnage. Certainly in 1955, against South Africa, he turned on a shattering display at Trent Bridge, taking 6 for 28—5 for 5 off 45 balls. But injury and lost form rendered his England appearances intermittent thereafter, and by the time he toured Australia a second time, in 1958–59, he was unexceptional. Bowling at Northampton was not the most uplifting experience for a fast bowler, but he had loyally resisted a suggestion that he attempt to transfer to Old Trafford, and he had always been aware that the life of an express bowler was the shortest of all.

Like Larwood before him, he moved to Australia, whose Test team he had once dismembered, and took up a teaching appointment in Melbourne, continuing to give something to the game with his perceptive radio and television commentaries and writing. To return to his book, he wrote with unnecessary modesty: 'Oh yes, there have been better fast bowlers.' (His opponents would not be convinced.) 'But I doubt whether there has been one who derived more pleasure from bowling fast. One of its greatest attractions for me is its straightforwardness. It is an honest pursuit whose rewards are gained by the sweat of the brow, and not by any underhand or surreptitious methods.'

15. ACTIONS PURE AND DUBIOUS

Alan Davidson—Ian Meckiff—Geoff Griffin—head injuries
assault with a dangerous weapon?—Wes Hall
Charlie Griffith—Pakistan and New Zealand fast men

The success of Hutton's team in Australia, built upon the
bowling of Tyson and Statham and the batting of May and
Cowdrey, with wonderful support from a number of others,
was cancelled out four years later when Benaud's team won
four Tests (by eight, eight, ten and nine wickets) and drew
the other. This crushing victory was made possible by solid
batting right down the order, splendid wicketkeeping by
Wally Grout, and devastating bowling in their contrasting
styles by Benaud, Davidson and Meckiff.

Davidson was a pure all-rounder, one of the finest ever.
Left-handed, he bowled over the wicket on and outside the
off stump, often with a grunt, always with deceptive movement in the air and off the seam. Ian Meckiff, who usually
opened the bowling with him, was a Victorian left-arm
bowler whose casual approach to the crease belied the speed
of his delivery. There was something unusual about his
action, and players and journalists, mainly from the English
camp, were convinced that his action was illegal. The sus-
picions were aired most loudly after Meckiff's 9 for 107 in
the second Test—'squealing' said Australia; 'compelled to
speak out at last' said England.

To add to England's woes, there were other bowlers about
with questionable actions. Gordon Rorke, an enormous and
handsome blond-haired 20-year-old, nicknamed 'Lothar',

dragged his rear foot some feet over the bowling crease and had a movement along his arm which may have been a strong wrist flick or a bending of the elbow. While he bowled the game entered near-stalemate, for the ball came down from such a height at such a pace that even the tallest batsman had difficulty in achieving more than a defensive prod off his chest. He conceded just over two runs per eight-ball over during the series. Then there was Keith Slater, sometimes off-spinner, sometimes medium-pacer. His action did not meet with general satisfaction, as neither did that of Jim Burke, chosen for his dour and courageous batting but occasionally called upon to 'bowl'. With his grotesque bent-arm off-breaks, he hit May's stumps when the England captain had scored 92 at Sydney.

Alan Davidson took 24 wickets in the series, Lindwall, in his final contest with England, seven, all taken with that familiar and skilful and roundarm and unquestionably fair delivery.

Meckiff tore tendons in an ankle, lost form and missed the 1961 tour of England, but—with a modified action—was back against South Africa in 1963–64, at Brisbane. There, on a December afternoon, umpire Colin Egar called him for throwing his second, third, fifth and ninth balls, and he was taken off at the end of the over, never to play first-class cricket again. Meckiff was a popular Australian, and won much sympathy among those who believed him innocent or to have been victimised in a 'clean-up' campaign. But he had been no-balled in two Sheffield Shield matches in the previous season by different umpires, which weakened the fairly common argument that since he had played all over Australia, South Africa, India, Pakistan and New Zealand without being 'called' his action must be legitimate.

It was another unhappy time for cricket and some of its participants. Elsewhere there were mutterings of illegal bowling actions—usually fast. Harold Rhodes of Derbyshire, who played twice against India in 1959 and upon whom much hope was pinned for his pace and hostility, was 'called' several times during the early 1960s. His elbow had an extended joint, which may have created an illusion, as did Statham's; but his action was unlike Statham's, and he was repeatedly under a cloud of controversy. In 1960 David 'Butch' White, a tearaway Hampshire bowler who was to play twice for England in Pakistan a year later, was also no-balled for throwing, thus rendering his future selection unlikely while the mood in international cricket was of purification.

The unhappiest incident of all, however, came at Lord's in 1960, when the young South African fast bowler Geoff Griffin was called for throwing by umpire Frank Lee eleven times during England's only innings, in which remarkably he also did the hat-trick. He had been 'called' in three earlier tour matches, and finished this Lord's Test wretchedly by being no-balled even during the exhibition match which followed the prematurely-ended Test match—firstly by Syd Buller for throwing then by Lee for not announcing that he was going to bowl underhand. Griffin, the first visiting bowler to be no-balled for throwing, saw out the tour, but was not called upon to bowl again.

There had been a faint precedent, when Cuan McCarthy, who had toured England with the 1951 South Africans, was 'called' in 1952, but he was then playing for Cambridge University. His action had caused some rumblings during the 1951 tour, when he came second in the bowling with 59 wickets, yet there were twin miseries awaiting the following year, when less than a fortnight before umpire Paddy Corrall no-balled him he struck Jim Langridge on the head with a ball which leapt off an irregularity in the pitch in the Sussex match at Hove. Langridge, who was almost 46, was knocked unconscious, his legs and arms twitching for a few moments. He was taken to hospital, and it is humorously recalled by some who were there that his first words upon regaining consciousness were, 'Was I out? Did I tread on my wicket?' Ever the professional. Robin Marlar, though, saw it as a tragedy, saying that 'Jim Langridge was killed by that blow on the temple, but it took him fourteen years to die. He became a very old man by the following season.'

There have been frequent cases of appalling head injury in modern cricket, all of them reminding those who play or watch—as if they needed reminding—that there is peril in fast bowling, and it is this peril which has a batsman's stomach aflutter as he ties on his thigh pad, slips in his protective box, buckles on his pads. It is this peril which has the spectators tensing on the edges of their seats, though they may not always be aware of it. So unaware can one become that the impact of ball on face or temple strikes shock through every single witness—a horrified surprise followed swiftly by the question: Why shock? It is an ever-present likelihood.

It was sickening when 20-year-old New Zealander John Sparling was knocked senseless at The Oval in 1958 by a ball from Trueman; it was enough to make hardened men weep when another New Zealander, the great left-hander Bert Sutcliffe, returned with split ear and bruised head bandaged after a blow from Adcock's fiery bowling at Ellis Park, Johannesburg at Christmas, 1953 to hit seven sixes in his 80 not out, accompanied in the last stages by Bob Blair, the Kiwi opening bowler, whose fiancée had been killed in a train disaster the day before; it was embarrassing when the same Sutcliffe, now 41, was floored by Trueman at Edgbaston in 1965; it left everyone despairingly helpless when West Indian Jackie Hendriks was removed to hospital for brain surgery after being struck by a ball from Graham McKenzie—no-one knew that night in Barbados in 1965 whether the batsman would live; it was horrifying when Nari Contractor, India's captain, was knocked senseless by a ball from Charlie Griffith into which he ducked during the match in Barbados in 1962 (he was hit on the back of the skull, which was fractured, and began to bleed from the nose; for many hours his life was despaired of, and Frank Worrell was among those who gave blood); it was an equally anxious time when Graeme Watson, hit on the bridge of the nose by a full-toss from Tony Greig in an

Australia v World XI match at Melbourne in 1972, was in an intensive-care ward for days, and received fourteen blood transfusions. He later ignored surgeons' advice never to play again. It was sad to see the prone figure of Duleep Mendis, the Sri Lanka batsman, after he had been hit in the centre of the forehead by a lifter from Australian speedster Jeff Thomson in the Prudential World Cup at The Oval in June, 1975, just as it was sad to see Sunil Wettimuny limping off with a badly bruised instep and ribs. From these recent incidents came two quotes accepted in good humour only since the batsmen seem to have recovered without ill effect. The first concerned the bowler, who was criticised for grinning at the collapsed Mendis. Thomson explained that he was tickled by what the batsman said and the way he said it: 'Oh God, I am going!' The second was related by Peter Marson of *The Times*, who wrote the following dialogue surrounding Wettimuny's arrival in hospital: 'What happened to you?' 'I was hit playing cricket.' 'Where?' 'At The Oval.' 'Who did it?' 'Thomson.' At this point, and with the timing peculiar to officers of the law, a police sergeant who had chanced to be within earshot of the conversation interjected: 'Do you wish to prefer charges?'

It raises an interesting point. A fast bowler who has written that he aims to hit batsmen could find himself in the position of an American ice hockey player who has recently faced a criminal charge of assault with a dangerous weapon (a hockey stick) during a match. The penalty, if convicted, is three years' jail.

The accident to Hendriks occurred during one of the stormiest of all Test series, when Australia's battered batsmen were forced to wear as much protection as they could comfortably amass in the face of the red-hot attack of Wes Hall and Charlie Griffith. England had discovered five years earlier just how difficult life could be on rock-hard Caribbean wickets against big, uninhibited fast bowlers who operated without restraint. The anxiety against Griffith was magnified by the conviction shared by many of his opponents that he threw the ball at least some of the time.

Hall had a magnificent, bounding approach, eyes bulging, teeth glinting, crucifix flying, climaxing in a classical cartwheel action and intimidating followthrough. An England batsman who had always regarded Hall with awe put him in the superhuman category when he saw him tumble as he bowled, skid on his elbows on the sandpaper surface, and pick himself up without a trace of bleeding. Griffith, who bowled viciously short at boyish Derek Underwood, batting number eleven in his first Test, and hit him in the teeth, in contrast to Hall, brought his large frame to the wicket at a fairly leisurely trot and swung his arm over at a low trajectory, the ball travelling at great speed and skimming towards the line of the batsman, making it hard for him to sway away from a short delivery. At the height of the controversy a number of players were outspoken, principally England's Ken Barrington, who batted bravely against all the hostile bowlers of his era and whose health suffered grievously, and also Norman O'Neill of Australia and Australia's captain turned journalist Richie Benaud. By his retirement, however, Griffith had been no-balled for throwing on two occasions only: by Cortez Jordan at Bridgetown shortly after the accident to Contractor, and by Arthur Fagg at Old Trafford during the 1966 West Indians' match against Lancashire.

Memories of Wesley Winfield Hall are of nothing if not glory. In 48 Tests he took 192 wickets and gave vast entertainment to millions through television or, more thrillingly, 'live'. He featured in one nail-biting finish after another: the tied Test at Brisbane, when his captain's last words to his tireless ace bowler were 'Whatever you do, don't bowl a no-ball!'; at Adelaide, when Mackay and Kline held out miraculously for an hour and a half to force a draw ('Slasher' Mackay taking Hall's final spitfire of a ball in the ribs and parading the bruise proudly for a week); at Lord's in 1963, when he broke Cowdrey's arm, and bowled the final over, his 40th of the innings, in one of the most pulsating draws of all time.

This latter match produced *two* of cricket's most stirring

innings, the first by Ted Dexter, whose first-innings 70 off 74 balls was noble, disdainful, furious in turn. At the start Griffith and Hall, in the words of Ian Wooldridge, 'like two huge hired assassins, seemed set for a bloodbath.' Reaching his fifty by smashing Griffith through the covers, Dexter's bat 'flashed through like a scimitar and the crack was like a British rifle sending death down into some deep, echoing gorge along the North-West Frontier'.

Later, in the second innings, when England needed 234 with time shrinking against rain interruptions, Brian Close almost pulled off a victory attempt of which even Jessop would have been proud. With not the least consideration for his safety, he waded into the West Indian fast attack, walking down the pitch before the ball had been released, swinging savagely, sometimes connecting, sometimes not. He was covered in ugly bruises and stitch marks by the time Murray caught him at the wicket off Griffith for 70. The match was a series of climaxes, and the last came when England, nine down and six short of victory, had two balls coming, with David Allen, the number ten, at strike, and Cowdrey, his arm in plaster, at the bowler's end. Hall could not break through with those final two deliveries, but the draw was universally pleasing, and West Indies' bowlers—'assassins' or not—were as vital to the saga as John Wilkes Booth or Sextus Tarquinius.

The speed attack of Hall and Griffith remains perhaps the most effective West Indies have ever had. After the war there had been Prior Jones, John Trim, Berkeley Gaskin, Hophnie Hines Johnson, Esmond Kentish, Gerry Gomez, Frank King, Tom Dewdney, Jaswick Taylor, Charlie Stayers, Lester King and Chester Watson. There had also been an electric little fast bowler named Roy Gilchrist—'Gilly', from Jamaica, who was sent home from a tour of India in 1958–59 for bowling 'beamers' (full-tosses around the batsman's head). He played in thirteen Tests, a significant number, for trouble surrounded him all the way, and even in the Lancashire League, where he took hundreds of wickets and numerous hat-tricks, he was never far from conflict and abuse.

Wes Hall's personality was such that no-one, not even the batsmen whom he bombarded, could take exception to him. Australia's Colin McDonald, whom Hall rated his most courageous opponent, presented him with his sweater, which had taken a horrible battering during the 1960–61 series. There were even instances where he eased the throttle against younger batsmen: Doug Walters was a case in point, receiving not one bouncer from Hall during his Sheffield Shield debut (when the West Indian was playing for Queensland). Hall's own wicketkeeper, Wally Grout, was not so lucky, having his jaw fractured by a wild delivery down the leg side.

Hall, who was timed at 91 mph at practice in Brisbane, was the first West Indian to take a Test hat-trick. It was at Lahore in 1958–59, and is the only Test hat-trick to be taken on an Easter Sunday. In that match, played on turf, Fazal Mahmood, who with Khan Mohammad had helped establish Pakistan cricket with their perplexing fast-medium bowling, was not effective. This was rare. He had taken nineteen wickets in the two preceding Tests, 13 for 114 against Australia at Karachi two years previously, and 12 for 99 in Pakistan's historic first victory over England at The Oval in 1954.

Pakistan had no pair to match Fazal and Khan Mohammad for over ten years after their retirement, but their problems with the new ball were never as acute as India's, for Saleem Altaf was a lively performer from 1967 to 1973, and the attack has recently been in the able hands of Asif Masood of the sweeping moustache and flowing hair and Sarfraz Nawaz, a huge uncomplicated man discovered as a net bowler and cast aside several times before he found a secure place in the Pakistan XI. His action is cumbersome but the major problem is usually the batsman's: he has to cope with a ball jabbed into the pitch and rising from near a length, with the giant Punjabi eyeing him unemotionally from his followthrough.

If appearances were all that mattered, New Zealand's Dick Collinge would be a world-beater. As it is, he has toured England four times, and has taken more wickets for his country than anyone except John Reid and the medium-pacers Bruce Taylor and Dick Motz (both of whom passed the hundred). Left-hander Collinge's sunny countenance was hidden by a large moustache during the 1975 Prudential World Cup competition, and his long Jumbo-Jet take-off, hands clawing menacingly at the air, strides seemingly long enough to take him clear over a roadway, brought him in some quality wickets.

Gary Bartlett had been one of the fastest bowlers produced by New Zealand, for whom he played ten times in the 1960s. But his action did not satisfy some purists. John Hayes, tall Tony MacGibbon, Harry Cave and Frank Cameron had earlier served their country well at home and abroad, and high hopes were held as the 1970s unpeeled for long-haired Murray Webb and broad-shouldered, hopping Bob Cunis. Dayle Hadlee, a rather slight figure, won regular success as a fast-medium bowler, and was joined in the side in 1973 by younger brother Richard, who was livelier still.

The leit-motif is, though, inescapable. Fast bowlers—really fast bowlers—preferably two, with a third of good class to provide support and breathing space, give a team ascendancy which often, early in a Test series, is so marked that the rest of the programme might just as well be cancelled, so one-sided can the combat become. Australia had such a combination in Lindwall and Miller, England in Trueman and Statham, and Statham and Tyson, West Indies in Hall and Griffith. Only months before their expulsion from Test cricket on political grounds, South Africa had it too in a pair of tall, fair-haired men, Peter Pollock and Mike Procter.

16. SPRINGBOKS—AND 'GARTH'

Peter Heine—Neil Adcock—Peter Pollock—Mike Procter
Graham McKenzie

During the 1950s England may have been rich in fast bowling, but South Africa's attack, having earlier been carried by Lindsay Tuckett, Eddie Fuller, Michael Melle, and McCarthy, was as hostile as any. In Neil Adcock and Peter Heine the Springboks had a pair strikingly similar in appearance and manner to Australia's slaughterers of the 1920s, Gregory and McDonald—the former open-faced, personable, rejoicing in his strength, the latter more tight-lipped, hard-eyed. In the thirteen Tests in which Adcock and Heine played together they took no fewer than 102 wickets and—of course—inflicted considerable physical damage. Heine, an Africaaner, and quite raw to international cricket, was a handful for any batsman, as Jim Laker recalled in his book *Over to Me* : 'Trevor Bailey's forward defensive stroke particularly annoyed Heine, and Trevor was at the receiving end of one of the most extraordinary speeches I ever heard on the cricket field. Halfway between a sneer and a growl, Heine said : "I want to hit you, Bailey ... I want to hit you over the heart." He meant every word of it. It was one hundred per cent pure malice. Heine once got me a stinging blow on the shoulder. He thought it was very funny, and asked : "Have I hurt you?" "I'll hit you over the head with the bloody bat if you do that again," was the best answer I could think up. Peter Richardson was hit on the head a couple of times by Heine, too, but he was careful to show

187

no sign of pain. It would have acted like blood to sharks.'

Adcock took 104 wickets in his 26 Tests, and one of the bowlers who gave tight support to him and Heine, and who was still of great value to South Africa when the next generation of fast men came, was left-handed all-rounder and sometime captain Trevor Goddard. By the early 1960s he was joined by Eddie Barlow, who was of immense value to the side as batsman, fast-medium bowler who could break irritating partnerships, lively fieldsman, and retailer of a bulldog spirit that helped blend the new Springbok talents together. In the home series of 1966–67 the surging South Africans, led by Peter van der Merwe, beat Australia three-one. In the third Test a 20-year-old Durban-born fast-bowling all-rounder named Mike Procter made his debut, taking seven wickets. In the next Test he took six more. And by the time Australia were in South Africa again three years later he had achieved such speed that 26 batsmen fell to his bowling in the four Tests, at an average of a mere 13·57. It was Australia's unhappiest series, for at the other end Peter Pollock took 15 at 17·20 to complete the domination.

The 1969–70 visitors were not without major batsmen: captain Lawry for years would have been in most people's World XI; Stackpole was a fearless hooker; Ian Chappell, unfortunately for him, at the start of the tour, was declared the best batsman in the world by his captain (Chappell made 92 runs in eight Test Innings); Walters had made 699 runs in six Test innings against the West Indies a year before; Redpath was highly respected; Sheahan was one of Australia's biggest hopes in years. What destroyed them to the tune of four massive defeats in four encounters? What had their batsmen ducking and weaving and adopting postures out of a Salvador Dali picture? Pace and bounce. After the weeks in India, where there had been hardships enough— though none stemming from fast bowling—the Australians simply could not cope with Procter and Pollock.

Pollock, brother of the great left-handed batsman Graeme, had a long, straight and time-consuming approach, with the ball held at his side and his knees coming up high. At the crease his hair was tossed back as he turned side-on, and the ball came over from a vigorous action. A Pollock bouncer sent John Edrich to hospital in 1965, when he lost sight of the ball in the Lord's Test. When Edrich's batting partner, Geoff Boycott, examined his swollen temple he offered the illuminating remark that 'it looks as if half the ball's in it!'

Procter bowled off a phenomenally long run, but though the walk back was tedious, it could be said for him that he ran in like an Olympic sprinter—and he *did* bowl fast. He bowled very fast, and off the wrong foot, that is to say, his right (bowling) arm and shoulder came round in the delivery, bringing the right leg as well, ridiculing orthodoxy. The rare action presented a new set of problems to batsmen, including that of judging the moment of delivery, usually uncomplicated (even if demanding) in the case of an orthodox bowler who wheels his arm over in tune with conventional wind-up and execution. Another poser set by Procter was how to deal with the alarming late in-dipper. In 1970, bowling for the Rest of the World against England at The Oval, Procter twice bowled Luckhurst for nought with balls that bent almost at right-angles from well outside off stump.

South Africa were outlawed by the rest of the cricketing nations after 1970, but Procter, like several of his teammates, found regular high-class competition in English county cricket, where for several seasons he lay claim to being the world's finest all-rounder. He batted magnificently, with strength and style; but it is as an extraordinary fast bowler that the world may well remember him. Batsmen who faced him at his sharpest will certainly never forget.

One of the more remarkable statistics to come from the 1969–70 South Africa v Australia rubber was Graham McKenzie's figures: one wicket for 333 runs in three Tests. For almost a decade he had been Australia's bowling backbone, beginning as a 20-year-old in the Lord's Test of 1961 (5 for 37 in the second innings), and banging down over after fiery over at home and in England, South Africa, West

Indies, India and Pakistan. He seemed tireless, for he was built like Goliath (he was actually nicknamed Garth after the sizable comic strip character) and he harnessed his great limbs and body into an economical run-up that seemed all ease and fluidity. His sturdy shoulders drove the ball with a smack into the pitch, and the lift off it was often too much for even the best batsmen in the world. Boycott's was just one forearm broken by his bowling.

His 246 Test wickets in sixty matches place him second in Australia's all-time list. Had he not been rested against weak opponents he would have topped the roll, and no more mild and pleasant man could have held the honour. He was the youngest ever to take 100, 150 and 200 Test wickets.

He joined Leicestershire in 1969, and for several seasons was the only Australian to be seen in county cricket, getting life from even the most placid pitches when least expected, and almost always being an awkward and sometimes dangerous bowler on a wicket retaining dew or rain.

McKenzie has never been a 'personality'; he is not surrounded by tales and legends; but he always had the respect of all players, and the Australian selectors, tempted by new talent, thought him finished with Test cricket some time before cricketers of other countries felt likewise.

He faded out during the 1970–71 series against England, when for the visitors John Snow's fast bowling had a decisive effect on the contest. McKenzie's relegation was without fanfare partly because of the heavy 'Snow-fall' and partly because of the arrival of a highly promising fellow Western Australian, Dennis Lillee.

17. SNOW'S SERIES

John Snow—incidents at Sydney—Bob Willis—also-rans
Garry Sobers

John Augustine Snow, a vicar's son, born in Peopleton, Worcestershire on October 13, 1941, has been one of cricket's enigmas, appearing to lose interest when play becomes quiet, and giving the impression—incomprehensible to some—that there is more to life than cricket. He joined Sussex as a batsman, but anyone who could whip the ball down at such speed with such striking movement off the seam had to have a future in the highest class of competition. When he made his England debut, against New Zealand at Lord's in 1965, he was a wiry 6 ft 1 in with close-cropped hair that gave him the head of a gladiator; by 1973, when the Test selectors lost interest in him, he was probably wirier still and carried a mass of tousled hair befitting a man who had issued two books of verse. In the meantime he had taken 176 wickets in 42 Tests, and contributed a great deal towards England's two-nil victory in Australia in 1970–71. (He took his 200th Test wicket in 1976.)

Of his 31 wickets in the six Tests, 24 were top-of-the-order batsmen, and his 7 for 40 to finish off the fourth Test, at Sydney, helped by thrilling two-handed diving catches by fellow fast bowlers Lever and Willis, was the realisation of a five-year threat. Australia's captain, left-handed Bill Lawry, withstood the onslaught gamely, carrying his bat for 60 in the innings of 116. McKenzie in what transpired to be his last Test appearance had to leave the field with blood streaming from his face after being hit by a Snow delivery which leapt off a length.

The England bowler was at the centre of the sensations at Sydney a month later during the final Test, which England had only to draw to win the Ashes. On the second evening one of his bouncers hit Jenner on the head, the helpless tail-ender turning away much as Tyson had done fifteen years previously to Lindwall. Snow's short-pitchers had created havoc throughout the series. Only the beefy Stackpole had hooked him with any conviction, and Walters, the prolific Walters, had been playing the bouncer like a blind man since the South African tour, sometimes lowering himself but leaving his bat up like a periscope. Occasionally Snow had bowled around the wicket, which made the lifter even more difficult to counter. It was probably a cumulative act of umpire Rowan's to warn Snow and his captain Illingworth after Jenner was felled.

Bowler and skipper did not take kindly to the official censure, and when Snow walked down to field at long leg, in front of the Paddington Hill, his shirt was grabbed by a spectator, and empty (most of them) beer-cans poured into the outfield. Before long Illingworth was leading his men from the field, and it took a restoration of peace among the spectators and a warning from the umpires that the match could be forfeited by England to bring the team back on the field. In their second innings Australia, needing 223 to win and level the series, lost Eastwood to Snow before a run had been scored, but England's key bowler then crashed into the fence in attempting to catch a hook by Stackpole, and the resultant dislocated finger saw him out of the match. This alone gave Australia great heart, but that evening they were 123 for 5, and Illingworth, D'Oliveira and Underwood bowled England to victory next morning by 62 runs. If one man ever influenced a series, however, it was the dark-haired fellow with his right hand in a sling awkwardly sipping champagne in a noisy, excited Sydney Cricket Ground pavilion on February 17, 1971.

Snow was a great success on his West Indian tour three

years earlier, taking 27 wickets at 18·66 in four Tests, including 7 for 49 at Kingston, 5 for 86 at Bridgetown, and 10 wickets in the match for 142 at Georgetown. As at The Oval in 1966, he took Garry Sobers's wicket first ball—this time with a shooter.

His mark, many times over, has been deeply imprinted on the game, but, as did the temperamental S. F. Barnes and the moody Keith Miller, he left observers wondering what might have been had he awoken every morning of his playing life with nothing on his mind but the ambition to bowl out all ten opponents before sunset. As he wrote in *Moments and Thoughts*, 'Maybe the oughts and countless thoughts best left in the thinker's head.'

As the 1975 season opened a new set of Test selectors put him back in England colours for the Prudential World Cup, but time was no longer on their—or his—side. Students of the game will argue for years yet whether Snow's presence in Australia in the 1974–75 series would have narrowed the gulf between the two sides.

There were fast bowlers enough in that MCC side: 34-year-old Lever; the promising fast-medium swing bowler Mike Hendrick; the reliable Geoff Arnold, than whom there has been no better fastish bowler in English conditions for some years; Chris Old, who with Arnold had blown India away for 42 in the Lord's Test that summer; Tony Greig, who could bowl fast-medium or off-spinners; and Bob Willis, probably the most promising of all the younger men.

Willis began with Surrey and moved to Warwickshire in 1972, having been flown to Australia during the 1970–71 tour to replace the injured Alan Ward. Willis was then just 21, a very tall, raw-boned, keen and agile cricketer who bowled with an awkward action off a long 'knees-up' run, and had an extra measure of speed. Ward's persistent injuries had hampered his career, which had been equally promising, to the point where he and his supporters were choking in exasperation. His stocks touched the depths in 1973 when his Derbyshire captain ordered him from the field when he was unwilling to start an afternoon spell of bowling. He left the staff, but returned the following season. Those who could recall the fire with which he bowled upon his 1969 Test debut saw it all as a major tragedy.

Robert George Dylan Willis, then, returning from Australia with damaged knees and undergoing operations in the spring of 1975, was looking dangerously like another dissipated English hope. Prayers were offered for the full physical recovery of the young man who had been England's one aggressive bowler in the face of the marauding 1973 West Indians and the fastest of the battery taken to Australia. His breakdown recalled the abortive career of the 6 ft 7 ins Northamptonshire bowler David Larter a decade earlier. He had never been free of injury for long. Nor had John Price, the rhythmic, heavily-built Middlesex bowler with the crescent run-up, who played fifteen times for England in eight years. Jeff Jones was another. The left-handed Welshman, who had bowled so valiantly in Australia and West Indies, was cruelly denied a long life in Test cricket by an elbow injury. His approach was long-strided, his action a robust pirouette, and in MCC's match against New South Wales during the 1965–66 tour he was banned from bowling again in the innings after running across the batsman's ground. His fifteen wickets in the Tests against Australia were more than anyone else took, with the brisk, hardworking David Brown (11) the only other England bowler to reach double-figures. Jones bowled most dangerously on hard pitches, and some of his sharpest performances were overseas. His angle of delivery made evasion difficult, and among those who failed to escape his lifters were the nimble Rohan Kanhai, whose cap flew off as he was hit over the heart, and Terry Jarvis, whose face needed fourteen stitches. 'It's terrifying, really,' Jeff Jones once wrote as he contemplated the speed of the ball.

Another who could extract high bounce from Australian wickets was Peter Loader, the long-limbed Surrey fast-medium bowler. Commentators were concerned during the 1958–59 series when, having changed to around-the-wicket. he dug one in which Australia's Burke could not avoid.

Fortunately the blow on his head was glancing. Loader, who, like Larwood and Tyson, settled happily in Australia, is the only England bowler to have taken a Test hat-trick since the war, dismissing West Indians Goddard, Ramadhin and Gilchrist at Headingley in 1957.

That 1957 tour was also the first made by Garfield Sobers, whose deeds as a batsman through two decades in every major cricket-playing country placed him on the highest pedestal and brought him a knighthood in 1975. Yet it ought never to be forgotten that with a new ball he could be a nightmare to any opening batsman. Curving it late and at high speed from his loose, springy run and whiplash delivery, he would have held his place in the West Indies XI for this ability alone.

Asked whom he would prefer to face from the fast men of the past ten years—Hall, Griffith, Sobers, Pollock, Procter, Snow, Willis, Ward, Lever, McKenzie—many an international batsman might have retorted that he would settle for a rainy day. Today's batsmen would probably feel the same about the chief bruisers of 1976: Lillee, Thomson, Roberts and Holding.

18. DEMONS OF TODAY

Thomson—Lillee—Roberts—Holding

'That was the greatest joke ever—just garbage!'

Jeffrey Robert Thomson was commenting on remarks attributed to him in a magazine article a few months earlier, in June of 1974. Then, in a series of quotes that had strangers smiling, cynically, unbelievingly, Thomson was alleged to have said, 'I enjoy hitting a batsman more than getting him out. It doesn't worry me in the least to see a batsman hurt, rolling around screaming and blood on the pitch.'

Barry Knight, the former England all-rounder, now living in Sydney, was quoted as having said of Thomson's bowling: 'It was the fastest I have encountered since Frank Tyson. He yorked four batsmen and knocked three others out of the game. He just went berserk.'

'Thommo' had been known to lose his temper. In 1972 he broke a soccer referee's nose with a straight left after disagreeing with a free-kick decision. He was banned for life 'for a while'. He loved his soccer, but there are other things in life, and he is never happier than when surfing or water-skiing. He took to rugby, and planned to take up baseball. He threw himself into a game of tennis early in 1975 and damaged his bowling shoulder; that cost him a Test appearance. At school he had been a javelin champion. At a sports carnival in a New South Wales country town he had been persuaded to try egg-throwing and easily outthrew the braggardly local champ only to have the new record nullified because no-one was standing far enough into the distance to catch the egg—a condition of the competition.

A section of the Press, after he had become a Test match star, concentrated on his love life. And shortly after the 1975 World Cup, in which his form had been disappointing, it was suggested that homesickness and the temporary loss of the joys of Australian outdoor (and indoor) life were affecting him. At one point his well-worn boots were blamed for a loss of rhythm. Whatever the cause, England's batsmen understandably could never be persuaded to forget the mauling they had sustained the previous winter.

Jeff Thomson was born in Bankstown, near Sydney, on August 16, 1950, and grew up to bowl with a similar action to that of his father, the right foot briefly passing behind the left in the delivery stride, the bowling arm cocking a long way behind the backside, the left leg kicking parallel to the turf. Thomson's broad shoulders take much of the strain as he catapults the ball, tumbling through to a short followthrough, long hair flying in a cock's comb.

He was timed in Melbourne at 88 mph, but claimed he was 'not flat out'. When cricket photographer Patrick Eagar measured speeds through a camera device in 1975, Thomson was the fastest of the chosen subjects at 90 mph, followed by Dennis Lillee at 89 mph, Andy Roberts (with a damaged finger, and bowling less fast than later in the day) 86 mph, Max Walker 79 mph, Bob Willis 75 mph, and Geoff Arnold 69 mph. None knew of the survey at the time.

During the Perth Test match of the 1975–76 series special tests carried out using photosonic camera equipment showed Thomson's speed at 99.688 mph, Roberts 93.6 mph, new bowler Holding 92.3 mph, and Lillee 86.4 mph. Senior lecturer in physical education at the Western Australian University, Tommy Penrose, who helped conduct the tests, said they should not be regarded as conclusive. One of his observations was that the ball slowed 'dramatically' after hitting the pitch. Once again one might search in vain for corroboration by a batsman.

Jeff Thomson, 6 ft and 13 stone, has bowled at such a

pace that batsmen could reasonably expect only to leave the wider ball alone and jab with hope at the straight one. All the alarmist talk of 1974 came true during the Test series that followed.

He had played once before for Australia—in 1972–73, his first season in first-class cricket—when his figures of none for 110 against Pakistan at Melbourne were understood upon the revelation that he had been playing despite a broken bone in the left foot. He had concealed the injury as he felt this could have been his one chance of an Australian cap, with so many rival fast bowlers around.

The quotes still came. When Colin Cowdrey, now 42, was flown out as a replacement batsman to the injury-stricken 1974–75 MCC side, Thomson is supposed to have said that 'he'll cop it too'. Though there was more of him to aim at, Cowdrey withstood the withering Australian fast attack gallantly, and was the first to hook the 'unhookable' Thomson—even though it was as late as the third Test, by which time he had taken his share of knocks, including one on exactly that part of his left forearm broken by Wes Hall a dozen years before.

Thomson is an easy-going fellow who could well exemplarise the proverbial reminder to the garrulous that God gave man *two* ears but only *one* mouth. He could well get as much satisfaction arresting wild pigs in the bush (part of his training) as dismissing batsmen, and there are some who feel his career will not be long—either because of what he takes out of himself or for his ease of distraction. Should this be so, his meteoric impression on the game will endure in legend.

His future was secured at the age of 25 when he signed a contract with Brisbane radio station 4IP which guaranteed him around £40,000 per annum for ten years. In a flash he became cricket's most expensive commodity.

About the same time, however, he was part of perhaps the most tragic irony in the history of fast bowling. A flatmate of his, Martin Bedkober, 23, who, like Thomson, had sought to advance his career by moving from Sydney to

Brisbane, was struck over the heart by a fast-medium ball while batting for Toombul in a club match against Sandgate-Redcliffe on December 13, 1975. He rubbed his chest for a few seconds, before collapsing. Players tried mouth-to-mouth resuscitation, but by the time ambulancemen arrived he had stopped breathing. Oxygen masks were tried but only a faint pulse in a thigh artery was detected. He was rushed to hospital but died inside a couple of hours. Blood had entered the pericardium, a sac surrounding the heart. He had recently undergone chest surgery but doctors said this in no way contributed to his death. Jeff Thomson attended his friend's funeral on his way back from the Perth Test match.

In recent seasons, the man who, apart from Thomson, has made Australian wicketkeeper Rod Marsh's life most uncomfortable has been Dennis Lillee, whose philosophy appeared unretractably in 1974 in his autobiography : 'I try to hit a batsman in the rib-cage when I bowl a purposeful bouncer, and I want it to hurt so much that the batsman doesn't want to face me any more. I want to be in complete control of the situation and that's one way of keeping hold of the reins. I don't want to hit a batsman on the head because I appreciate what damage that can do.'

He claims—with clear justification—that he is expressing what most fast bowlers have been afraid to reveal, and if forthrightness in itself warrants applause then Lillee is entitled to some handclaps for his remarks.

Dennis Keith Lillee was born in Perth on July 18, 1949, and found early inspiration in Wes Hall's athleticism. Lillee's name first attracted the world's attention when he took 5 for 84 in his Test debut at Adelaide against England. It was a relief to Australians to see someone getting results after the disappointment of 'Froggy' Thomson. When English-born left-arm fast bowler Tony Dell joined Lillee in the attack for the final Test of that 1970–71 series it seemed Australia might settle down at last.

Dell was discarded, but Lillee cemented his place in the side with an astonishing 8 for 29 next season against a

World XI on the lightning-fast Perth wicket. He had felt off-colour after a few overs, but Ian Chappell persuaded him to have another over, and then another, and in fifteen balls he took a further six wickets for no runs. Among his victims were Gavaskar, Engineer, Clive Lloyd, Greig, Sobers, and Richard Hutton. He had bowled every ball as fast as he could ... and learned that life could be short if he stuck to this principle. A thoughtful man, he never stopped learning that season or the next, when he toured England.

Later in the World XI series he broadened his education further by bowling to Garry Sobers as he put together a magnificent 254 at Melbourne, straight-driving Lillee's yorkers, and some deliveries 'on the up', back past the tumbling bowler to the sightscreen.

In England, after a season in the Lancashire League, Lillee, complete with a Mephistophelean moustache, was constantly threatening, and finished with a record 31 wickets in the five Tests of 1972, including a proud ten in the last, won by Australia to level the series. What was not generally appreciated was that the nagging back pains came from a seriously damaged spine. He bowled gallantly against Pakistan in the following home season, and went with Australia to West Indies. There the back gave way completely, and it was left to Max Walker ('Tangles', the very tall Tasmanian with the odd 'no-left-arm' action) and Jeff Hammond, the young, vigorous South Australian, to carry the side's pace attack—a task they performed heroically.

With four stress fractures at the base of his spine, there were few willing to bet that Lillee would play Test cricket again. Little account was taken of his burning desire to overcome the near-crippling disability. He spent six weeks in a plaster cast, resumed light training, and built up to a state of fitness where he could play as a batsman. Eventually he tried bowling—at medium pace—and there were no twinges. His training was intensified—hours upon countless hours of feverish dedication away from the public gaze. The season of 1973–74 saw him as simply a club cricketer.

Then came the important 1974–75 season, with England

landing for a six-Test series in defence of the Ashes. Lillee pronounced himself fully fit, and the moment of fulfilment came as he took the field at Brisbane in the first Test with his new, relatively unknown partner Jeff Thomson. By the end of the rubber—in fact after two Tests—their names had become synonymous with pain and terror or triumph and victory, dependent upon one's nationality.

Lillee took two wickets in each of England's first eight innings in the series, and then increased his output to four in each innings of the fifth Test, at Adelaide. In the sixth Test he was forced to withdraw after six overs with a damaged foot, but he had in that brief spell inflicted on England's current top batsman Dennis Amiss his third successive Test duck, having had him caught twice at Adelaide.

Lillee's mark, embellished by a relationship with the chanting crowds worthy of a prizefighter's and by some red-hot verbal exchanges and gesticulations to and from his opponents in the middle, had been made strong and clear. He was back, with a beautifully-controlled nineteen-pace approach, almost as fast as the pre-breakdown model and considerably more clever. When he took 5 for 34 against Pakistan at Headingley in Australia's opening Prudential Cup match in 1975 he rated comparison with Lindwall.

Observers could not be so assured when West Indians Kallicharran and Lloyd thrashed him in the later round and the Lord's final. Was the back repair holding? Could he still dictate a Test series?

He could. His 21 England wickets in the four Tests of the 1975 series were five more than the next-highest—Thomson (16). In less than a year the pair had taken 95 England wickets. In the home series which came next, against West Indies, Lillee took 27 wickets, Thomson 29.

The West Indians, either side of a crushing innings victory at Perth, were utterly demoralised by the Australian pace attack, and lost the series 5–1. They lost blood too. Alvin Kallicharran, the boyish left-hander, had his nose broken by a Lillee bouncer and later was sick by the side of the pitch after being struck resoundingly on the back of the head by a ball from Thomson (who was later quoted as saying that the time for protective headgear had now come —a call echoed by wicketkeeper Marsh).

Australia has a good stock of reserves—left-arm swinger Gary 'Gus' Gilmour, fast right-arm Victorian Alan Hurst, ever-reliable Max Walker, young South Australian tearaway Wayne 'Fang' Prior. Indeed, her cricketers have been fervently wishing that the politicians had not kept Australia from touring outlawed South Africa, for the odds were propitious that Lillee, Thomson and company might be exacting spectacular revenge for the drubbing of 1969–70.

In the matter of fire-power in 1975, there was just one challenger from afar. This was Andy Roberts, who, with fellow West Indians Boyce, Julien, and Holder, formed one of cricket's best all-round fast attacks. Boyce had shattered England in 1973 with his fast-motion gazelle-like approach fellow West Indians Boyce, Julien, and Holder, formed one of the most challenging bowlers in the game, bringing the ball in and up at above medium pace. Julien had much of Sobers about him, taking great raking strides and bowling lively left-arm swingers. But of them all, Anderson Montgomery Everton Roberts, born January 29, 1951, one of a fisherman's large family on the tiny island of Antigua, was the fastest. He was so fast that his name was made in a matter of weeks as he emerged from nowhere, via a coaching course at Alf Gover's school, to the Hampshire staff. Playing a qualifying season in the second eleven, he took 40 wickets and hurt a lot of batsmen.

He got down to real business in 1974, when he played in the County Championship on the generally slow pitches against some of the world's greatest batsmen. He took 119 wickets at 13.62 to head the national averages. A worrying knee injury of two years previously showed no sign of recurrence as he quietly went about his job of helping Hampshire to retain the title—something they ultimately failed to achieve, finishing two points behind Worcestershire as they waited hopelessly for the rain to stop during what would have been their last match of the season.

Roberts has a moderately long run to the wicket, building up his speed rapidly. His arm comes over at right-angles to his torso, but reaches a height as his left shoulder dips. He glides along on his right toecap and hits the crease area with all his weight. His speed through the air is undoubtedly close to the maximum man can expect to attain; the ball's characteristic movement is from off to leg, but his away-swinger is impressive. With the steep lift he obtains, the physical peril is unusually high. Just to make life harder for batsmen, he has a fast bouncer and a slower one, the latter aimed at encouraging the hook shot. So fast does the ball come through that even such a skilful fielder as Gordon Greenidge sometimes wears a protective box when stationed at slip to Roberts. It was Hampshire club-mate Greenidge's dropped catch that cost Roberts a hat-trick in the Old Trafford Test of 1976, a match in which he three times took two wickets with consecutive balls.

Roberts, who took his 100th Test wicket in only his 19th Test, dislikes batsmen ducking into his bowling, and does not enjoy in the least seeing opponents struck about the head. But it is part of his professional attitude that such an incident has to be pushed behind him instantly. He is outwardly unemotional, and it is probably this quality that gives him the most sinister aspect of all today's fast men. 'A cold killer' is how one county player referred to him—in awe, not out of revulsion.

He played cricket non-stop for several years—Tests, tours, and for Hampshire—causing concern to West Indian administrators lest he burn himself out years ahead of time; but in 1976 a deadly partner was found for him. Michael Anthony Holding, from Jamaica, born February 16, 1954, showed promise in Australia, and within months he had torn India apart and devastated England. A former track athlete, Holding, tall and sparely-built, has a long, lithe, lissom run-up, elbows pumping like a dancer's, head reared as if to delight in the zephyr resulting from his own fleetness. His gyratory action climaxes in an apparently effortless release of a ball that blurs its bouncing way to the other end at a ferocious speed. At Old Trafford in 1976 his attack upon 45-year-old Test recall Brian Close sent deep recoils through that tough man's frame and shivers through onlookers. At The Oval a month later he took fourteen England wickets—nine bowled, three lbw, two caught behind the wicket. No West Indies bowler had taken fourteen wickets in a Test or matched his 8 for 92 in the first innings. The pitch was perfect throughout. Only sadists preferred the intimidation at Manchester to the supreme exhibition of fast bowling skills at Kennington.

Holding's attack upon Bishan Bedi's India at Kingston in the last Test of the 1975–76 series had led to a kind of desperate capitulation by Bedi—a declaration at 306 for 6 (with two retired hurt) in the first innings, when he felt his last three batsmen would be in danger of serious injury, and a concession that five out (for 97) was all out in the second innings. West Indies, needing a mere thirteen runs, won by ten wickets. In India's first innings Gaekwad (81) was hit stunningly on the left ear and Viswanath (8) had a finger broken, both by Holding's bowling; Patel (14) needed stitches to a facial cut after being hit by Holder. None of them batted further in the match. Bedi and Chandrasekhar were injured in the field. This infamous match cut short the memory of India's glorious preceding victory at Port of Spain, when they made a record 406 runs to win by six wickets.

Roberts and Holding thus arrived in England in the spring of 1976 with a menacing reputation. When the junior fast bowler in the West Indies party—Wayne Wendell Daniel, from Barbados, born as recently as January 16, 1956, due to play for Middlesex in 1977—stepped (heavily) into the Test side, England were faced with probably the fastest *trio* of bowlers ever working together. Young Daniel, moving 26 paces to the crease as though wading through knee-high water, is wildly inaccurate at times but lethal when on target. There was no relief. The over rate was appallingly slow, so none of the three ever faced the prospect of being bowled to exhaustion. The consequent run rate, which was inescapably low, was an added pressure upon batsmen. David Steele, England's grim-faced hero of 1975, began with a century, but thereafter was scorched from the scene, victim of an irresistible impulse to hook. The lofty Greig was repeatedly yorked. Veterans Edrich and Close needed more than just valour to cope with the merciless onslaught.

It was the physical threat of Roberts, Lillee, and Thomson that had prompted the Pakistan Board of Control in 1975 to call for a special sitting of the International Cricket Conference before the Prudential World Cup in order to examine intimidatory bowling, its interpretation and prevention. The special regulation brought in at that meeting was that any ball passing over the batsman's head (judged by his normal stance position, i.e. not when he is ducking) would be called 'wide'. Every fast bowler knows—as for that matter does every batsman—that the ball sailing over the head ought to be harmless. It is the ball at the cheekbone or collarbone that threatens survival. Nevertheless, the tournament was played out fairly free of incident, though there were sporadic calls by umpires for 'overhead wides'. The experiment may some day be broadened to include Test or other first-class matches. Then its futility may be seen.

A year later, following the West Indies–India series (and also a close call for Lancashire's David Lloyd, who was bloodily knocked cold by a ball from Northants and England fast bowler Bob Cottam at the start of the 1976 season), the ICC again pronounced upon intimidatory bowling, this time expressing disapproval, and condemning in particular beamers and the bowling of bouncers at 'non-recognised' batsmen. This led to hilarious suggestions that lower-order batsmen should wear 'NRB' badges. How long, it was asked, need a batsman stay in before shedding the 'non-recognised' label?

Much blood has been spilt on cricket pitches all around

the world, at first-class and junior levels—and a thimbleful would have been that much too much. Avoidance of injury should not be a component of sport, but until a soft ball replaces the traditional hard $5\frac{1}{2}$ oz leather job, or until human nature is somehow rendered infallibly and horribly uniform, fast bowlers will, by design or otherwise, batter and bruise.

As to whether the dangers are greater today than in past eras, measurable sporting achievement has improved, almost without exception, throughout this century. Over 250 Olympic records were shattered in the 1976 Games. Why should not bowlers be faster than their forebears? Don Fair pointed out, in a letter to *The Times* (July 15, 1976), that average man, 5 ft $4\frac{3}{4}$ ins in 1700, is now 5 ft 9 ins. Thirty years ago the larger bottoms of Eton schoolboy oarsmen forced the abandonment of the traditional boats in favour of more spacious vessels. Mr Fair claimed that the cricket pitch should now be $23\frac{1}{2}$ yards long, with an extension hereafter of 0.17 inches per decade. 'The dimensions of the traditional cricket pitches,' he wrote, 'are now suitable only for English women cricketers (average height 5 ft 4 ins) and perhaps some Asiatic peoples.'

Gavaskar and Viswanath, to think of but two, might demur at the postscript.

Meanwhile, batsmen have the choice of swaying to safety, as Reg Simpson did, or hitting the devils back over their heads, as Charlie Macartney and George Gunn liked to do. They could, alternatively, pad their bodies and take on the appearance of Michelin men at the crease, or wear crash-helmets and, with new-found confidence, as Tony Greig thinks could happen, hook the bouncers out of the ground, thrilling all but the bowler.

The next few years will tell. There are those of us who feel that the enchanting art of spin bowling cannot finally perish, and that there will be a revival. Should there be, then the recurring hysteria over the dangers of fast bowling will diminish until such time as another John Jackson or Kortright or Knox or Gregory or Larwood or Miller or Tyson or Griffith or Thomson or Lillee or Roberts or Holding appears. Then the humanitarians will have their sleepless nights, and so will the batsmen. Then the editors will call for their boldest headline type. Then the team without armament—forgetting the times when it had armament—will call for moderation. And then, one would suppose, the ground will be full, as it was when the Christians, without even $4\frac{1}{4}$ inches of willow, took guard to the lions.

MAIN SOURCES

Altham, H. S. *A History of Cricket* (Allen & Unwin)

Arlott, John *Fred: Portrait of a Fast Bowler* (Eyre & Spottiswoode); (ed.) *From Hambledon to Lord's: The Classics of Cricket* (Christopher Johnson)

Barker, Ralph *Ten Great Bowlers* (Chatto & Windus)

Beldam, G. W. & Fry, C. B. *Great Bowlers and Fielders: Their Methods at a Glance* (Macmillan)

Brittenden, R. T. *Great Days in New Zealand Cricket* (Bailey Bros & Swinfen)

Chignell, W. R. *A History of the Worcestershire County Cricket Club* (Littlebury)

Coldham, J. D. *Northamptonshire Cricket: A History* (Heinemann)

Cricket: A Weekly Record of the Game

Crowley, Brian; Duffus, Louis & Parker, A. C. *Currie Cup Story* (Nelson)

Daft, Richard *A Cricketer's Yarns* (Chapman & Hall)

Foster, Frank R. *Cricketing Memories* (London Publishing)

Fry, C. B. *The Book of Cricket* (Newnes)

Grace, W. G. *Cricket* (Arrowsmith)

Harris, Lord *A Few Short Runs* (Murray)

James, C. L. R. *Beyond a Boundary* (Hutchinson)

Laker, Jim *Over to Me* (Muller)

Larwood, Harold *Bodyline?* (Elkin Mathews & Marrot); *The Larwood Story* (with Kevin Perkins) (Allen)

Lillee, Dennis *Back to the Mark* (as told to Ian Brayshaw) (Hutchinson)

Lillywhite, Frederick *Cricket Scores and Biographies of Cele-*

brated Cricketers, Vols I and II

Martineau, G. D. *The Field is Full of Shades* (Sporting Handbooks); *They Made Cricket* (Museum Press)

Morrah, Patrick *Alfred Mynn and the Cricketers of his Time* (Eyre & Spottiswoode)

Moyes, A. G. *Australian Bowlers* (Harrap)

'Old Ebor' *Old English Cricketers* (Blackwood)

Peebles, Ian *Straight from the Shoulder* (Cricketer/Hutchinson)

Tyson, Frank *A Typhoon Called Tyson* (Heinemann)

Whitington, R. S. & Hele, George *Bodyline Umpire* (Rigby)

Wisden Cricketers' Almanack

Wooldridge, Ian *Cricket, Lovely Cricket* (Hale)

Wynne-Thomas, Peter *Nottinghamshire Cricketers 1821–1914*

INDEX

212

213

214

218

THE POCKET CALCULATOR GAME BOOK
by EDWIN SCHLOSSBERG *and* JOHN BROCKMAN

FIFTY FASCINATING NUMBER GAMES AND PUZZLES you can play with the newest electronic wonder!

The pocket calculator—the gadget that revolutionized the business world . . . and has now become an intriguing toy. This book contains rules for fifty games using calculators, to play with other competitors or just by yourself, for fun or as a learning aid. . . .

Play Poker, Calculator Solitaire or Maze Runner—or try some of the more exotic ones like Mind Control, Lover's Maze or Fast Eddie. This book can turn your calculator into a game board, a puzzle board and a deck of cards!

0 552 98005 6—**85p**

A WAY OF LIVING AS A MEANS OF SURVIVAL
by MICHAEL WHEATLEY

'At last an up-to-date, comprehensive encyclopedia of health. A way of eating, thinking and living. A philosophy as well as a practical guide.'

In this book, Michael Wheatley gives the basic facts about:
NUTRITION: the foods you need to keep your body healthy. . . .

DISEASES: how health foods can help you overcome them —and avoid them. . . .

HAPPINESS: true happiness comes only through good health. . . .

SEX: good health is a vital factor in your sex life. . . .

HEALTH FOODS: a guide to buying, cooking and eating. . . .

0 552 10337 3—**85p**

BRUCE TEGNER'S COMPLETE BOOK OF JUDO

NOW! A NEW METHOD OF LEARNING THE
THRILLING SPORT OF JUDO!!
YOU DO NOT HAVE TO MAKE JUDO A 'WAY
OF LIFE' TO ENJOY ITS MANY BENEFITS.

All the techniques needed to progress from beginner to
Black Belt are taught in this book; in addition, there is a
section of basic self-defence which can be learned by ANY-
BODY.

Bruce Tegner faithfully follows the original ideas of the
founder of Judo, Dr. Jigaro Kano, adapting those ideas to
the needs of twentieth-century people.

0 552 07917 0—**65p**

BRUCE TEGNER'S COMPLETE BOOK OF JUKADO

JUKADO COMBINES THE FUN AND EXCITEMENT
OF A SPLENDID PHYSICAL RECREATION
ACTIVITY WITH PRACTICAL TECHNIQUES OF
EFFECTIVE, MODERN SELF-DEFENCE.

Bruce Tegner presents, for the first time in published form,
his original system of grade ranking in his modern version
of Jiu Jitsu which he has named JUKADO. In JUKADO,
utility and pleasure are joined; there are good, simple,
workable defences selected mainly from Judo, Karate and
Aikido, and there is the pleasure of attaining achievement
goals as you progress through the work required for grading
each rank—from White to Black Belt.

Whether you are a beginner, an experienced enthusiast, or a
teacher you will find this book of great value and interest.
This title, an original and brilliant contribution, is Bruce
Tegner's 22nd book in the field of the unarmed fighting
arts for sport, self-defence and recreation.

0 552 08456 5—**65p**

A SELECTED LIST OF SPORTS BOOKS
FROM CORGI

All these books are available at your bookshop or newsagent: or can be ordered direct from the publisher. Just tick the titles you want and fill in the form below.

....

CORGI BOOKS, Cash Sales Department, P.O. Box 11, Falmouth, Cornwall.

Please send cheque or postal order, no currency. **U.K. Customers** allow 19p for the first book, plus 9p per copy for each additional book ordered, to a maximum charge of 73p. **B.F.P.O. and Eire** allow 19p for the first book, plus 9p per copy for the next 6 books, thereafter 3p per book. **Overseas Customers** allow 20p for the first book and 10p per copy for each additional book.

NAME (Block letters)   ....

ADDRESS   ....

(APRIL 77)   ....

While every effort is made to keep prices low, it is sometimes necessary to increase prices at short notice. Corgi Books reserve the right to show new retail prices on covers which may differ from those previously advertised in the text or elsewhere.